RANDIE
Oct 14/04

LOVE

Rhonda
+
Bob

HAPPY BIRTHDAY

Weihnachten 1979

BREADS OF THE WORLD
AN EASY-TO-BAKE COLLECTION
FROM 46 COUNTRIES

BREADS OF THE WORLD

AN EASY-TO-BAKE COLLECTION FROM 46 COUNTRIES

Mariana Honig

1977
CHELSEA HOUSE PUBLISHERS
New York, London

Design: Susan Lusk
Managing Editor: Laurie Likoff
Project Editor: Ingrid Russell
Illustrator: Gordon Nelson

Library of Congress Cataloging in Publication Data

Honig, Mariana, 1940-
    Breads of the world.

    1. Bread. I. Title.
TX769.H68   641.8'15   77-7208
ISBN 0-87754-051-9

CHELSEA HOUSE PUBLISHERS

Harold Steinberg, Chairman & Publisher,   Andrew E. Norman, President
Susan Lusk, Creative Director
A Division of Chelsea House Educational Communications, Inc.
70 West 40th Street New York, N.Y. 10018

For Erik, Alexander and Amanda

TABLE OF CONTENTS

1
BREAD / YESTERDAY AND TODAY
PAGE 1

2
INGREDIENTS AND UTENSILS
PAGE 11

3
TIPS ON BAKING
PAGE 23

4
WHAT WENT WRONG
PAGE 29

5
SAVORY BREADS WITH YEAST

Peda Bread, *Armenia,* 37
Kartoffelbrot, *Austria,* 38
New Brunswick Oatmeal Bread,
    Canada, 39
Hua Chuan (Rolls), *China,* 41
Pan De Cuba De Afuera Dura, *Cuba,* 42
Kartoffelbrød, *Denmark,* 44
Sour Bread, *Denmark,* 45
Barley Bread, *Egypt,* 47
Wheat Bread, *Egypt,* 48
Graham Squares, *England,* 50
Honey Bread, *Ethiopia,* 52
Buckwheat Bread, *Finland,* 53
Finnish Rye Bread, *Finland,* 54
French Bread, *France,* 55

French Country Rye Bread, *France,* 57
Gannat Bread, *France,* 59
Walnut Bread from Burgundy, *France,* 60
Zwiebel Kuchen, *Germany,* 61
Karin's Whole-wheat Bread, *Iceland,* 63
Barbari Bread, *Iran,* 65
Pane Origano, *Italy,* 66
Pizza, *Italy,* 68
Pizza Napoletana, *Italy,* 69
Pizza Con Funghi, *Italy,* 69
Pizza Con Cipolle Ed Olive, *Italy,* 70
Challah, *Jewish,* 71
Whole-wheat Anise and Sesame Seed
    Bread, *Morocco,* 73
Sfenj (Doughnuts), *Morocco,* 74

Lefse, *Norway,* 75
Sabina Bread, *Poland,* 77
Broa, *Portugal,* 78
White Bread, *Portugal,* 79
Alma's Black Bread, *Russia,* 80
Scandinavian White Bread,
　　Scandinavia, 82
Fullkornsbröd, *Sweden,* 84
Kryddlimpa, *Sweden,* 85
Rågkakor, *Sweden,* 87
Sur-sött Bröd, *Sweden,* 89

Tunnbröd, *Sweden,* 90
Pumpkin Bread, *Trinidad,* 92
Dill Bread, *United States,* 93
Plain All-purpose Yeast Dough,
　　United States, 94
Herb Bread, *United States,* 95
Ruth's Peanut Butter Bread,
　　United States, 97
Ruth's Pear and Date Bread,
　　United States, 99
Seven Grain Bread, *United States,* 100

6
SAVORY ROLLS & BUNS WITH YEAST

Kaisersemmeln, *Austria,* 103
Paezinhos De Cerveja, *Brazil,* 105
Karlsbad Buns, *Czechoslovakia,* 106
Cheese Baps, *England,* 108
Croissants, *France,* 109
Pogacsa, *Hungary,* 111
Grissini, *Italy,* 113
Small Poppy Seed Braids, *Jewish,* 115
Zemmeln, *Jewish,* 117
Onion Zemmeln, *Jewish,* 118
Margaret's Sambosas, *Kenya,* 119
Fatayir, *Lebanon,* 121
Panecillos, *Mexico,* 123

Khboz Bishemar, *Morocco,* 124
Kringler, *Norway,* 126
Bergis, *Sweden,* 127
Frukostgifflar, *Sweden,* 129
Chicken Borek, *Turkey,* 130
English Muffins, *United States,* 131
Georgia Raised Biscuits,
　　United States, 133
Cloverleaf Rolls, *United States,* 134
Parker House Rolls, *United States,* 135
Pretzels, *United States,* 136
Southern Potato Rolls, *United States,* 137

7
SWEET BREADS WITH YEAST

Faschingskrapfen, *Austria,* 141
Omilla's Buchteln, *Austria,*
Czechoslovakia, 143
Sour Cream Dough,
　　Austria, Hungary, Rumania, 145
Striezel, *Austria,* 147
Topfen Kuchen, *Austria,* 149
Viennese Kugelhupf, *Austria,* 150
Zwetschkenkuchen, *Austria,* 152
Verviers Bread, *Belgium,* 154
Fruit Bread, *Brazil,* 156
Canadian Raisin Bread, *Canada,* 158
Mährischer Kuchen, *Czechoslovakia,* 159
Chelsea Buns, *England,* 160
Hot Cross Buns,
　　England, United States, 162
Pope Ladies, *England,* 164
Pulla, *Finland,* 165

Baba au Rhum or Romovaya Baba,
　　France, Russia, 167
Chocolate Buns, *France,* 169
Berliner, *Germany,* 171
Oliebollen, *Holland,* 172
Rusks, *Holland,* 174
Barm Brack, *Ireland,* 176
Maritozzi Romani, *Italy,* 177
Panettone, *Italy,* 178
Pangiallo, *Italy,* 180
Julekake, *Norway,* 182
Vaniljboller, *Norway,* 184
Walnut and Poppy-seed Bread,
　　Poland, 186
Massa Sovada, *Portugal,* 188
Portuguese Sweet Bread, *Portugal,* 190
Kulich, *Russia,* 191
Ukrainian Coffee Bread, *Russia,* 193

Blåbärskaka, *Sweden*, 195
Bullar, *Sweden*, 197
Fettisdagsbullar, *Sweden*, 199
Kanelbrod, *Sweden*, 201
Kryddskorpor, *Sweden*, 203
Lussekatter, *Sweden*, 205

Saffron Cardamon Braid, *Sweden*, 207
Skokladgiffel, *Sweden*, 209
Slottskringlor, *Sweden*, 211
Birnenwecken, *Switzerland*, 212
Bourbon Sticky Buns, *United States*, 214
Cinnamon Rolls, *United States*, 216

8
SOURDOUGH BREADS

Sourdough Starter, 221
Sourdough French Bread, *France*, 222
Schwarzwalder Roggen Brot,
    Germany, 223
Baltic Rye Bread, *Lithuania*, 224
Medeltida Bröd, *Sweden*, 226

Plain White Sourdough Bread,
    United States, 227
Sourdough Butter Rolls,
    United States, 228
Sourdough Pancakes, *United States*, 229

9
SAVORY QUICK BREADS

Bannock, *Canada*, 233
Marylo Velasco's Empanadas Chilenas,
    Chile, 234
Fladbrød, *Denmark*, 236
Scones, *England*, 237
Bacon Barley Bread, *Finland*, 238
Gougère, *France*, 239
Laufabraud, *Iceland*, 241
Chapati, *India*, 243
Mrs. Mendiratta's Lentil Chapati,
    India, 244
Cumin Balls, *India*, 245
Well-behaved Bread, *India*, 246
Banbridge Oatcakes, *Ireland*, 247
Jack and Doris Smith's Irish Soda Bread,
    Ireland, 248

Corn Bread, *Mexico*, 249
Potato Lefse, *Norway*, 250
Barra Muffins, *Scotland*, 251
Oatcake, *Scotland*, 252
Surmjölksbröd, *Sweden*, 253
Boston Brown Bread, *United States*, 254
Cornsticks, *United States*, 255
Cream Cheese Biscuits,
    United States, 256
New England Bran Muffins,
    United States, 257
Popovers, *United States*, 258
Southern Sweet Potato Bread,
    United States, 259
Spoon Bread, *United States*, 260

10
SWEET QUICK BREADS

Citrus Bread, *Barbados*, 263
Corn Bread, *Caribbean*, 264
Pumpkin Bread, *Caribbean*, 265
Currant Muffins, *England*, 266
Lemon Bread, *England*, 267
Honey Bread, *Holland*, 268
Breakfast or Tea Bread, *India*, 269
Poori with a Sweet Filling, *India*, 270
Liberian Rice Bread, *Liberia*, 271
Hastbullar, *Sweden*, 272

Pepparkaka, *Sweden*, 273
Spicy Almond Bread, *Turkey*, 275
Blueberry Muffins, *United States*, 276
Corn Muffins with Orange,
    United States, 277
Philpy, *United States*, 278
Pecan Bread, *United States*, 279
Rice Bread, *West Africa*, 280
Beogradska Pita, *Yugoslavia*, 281

11
PANCAKES AND WAFFLES

Basic Recipe for Thin Pancakes, 285
Basic Mix for Pancakes and Waffles,
    American-Style (I), 286
Palatschinken, *Austria,* 287
Pfannkuchen fur Suppe,
    Austria, Germany, 288
Crepes Flambé, *France,* 289
Thin Pancakes with Meat, Sea Food or
    Vegetable Filling, *Europe,*
    United States, 290

Blinis, *Finland, Russia, Sweden,* 291
Crepes Suzette, *France,* 292
Scripelle, *Italy,* 293
Blintzes, *Jewish,* 294
Gräddvafflor, *Sweden,* 295
Morotspannkakor, *Sweden,* 296
Plattar, *Sweden,* 297
Coconut Pancakes, *Thailand,* 298
Pancakes or Waffles American–Style (II),
    United States, 299

12
SANDWICHES

Danish Beef Tartare Sandwich,
    Denmark, 303
Shrimp Sanwich, *Denmark,* 304
Croûte Suisse, *France,* 305
Croque-Monsieur, *France,* 306
Croque-Madame, *France,* 306
Mussel Sandwich from Provence,
    France, 307
Checkerboards, *Germany,* 308

Guastieddi, *Italy,* 309
Mozzarella in Carrozza, *Italy,* 310
Appelkalle, *Sweden,* 311
Caviar Sandwich, *Sweden,* 312
Grilled Salami Sandwich, *Sweden,* 313
Grilled Swiss Cheese Sandwich,
    .. *Sweden,* 314
Ölsmorgas, *Sweden,* 315

13
WHAT TO DO WITH LEFTOVER BREAD

Honeycake, *Arabic,* 319
Mock Devonshire Cream, *Arabic,* 319
Mohr im Hemd, *Austria,* 320
Mutti' Semmel Knodeln, *Austria,* 322
Bread Pudding, *France,* 323
Picatostes, *Spain,* 324
Spanish Toast, *Spain,* 325

Fattigmans Middag, *Sweden,* 326
Swiss Apple and Bread Dessert,
    Switzerland, 327
Garlic-Parmesan Bread,
    United States, 328
Italian-style Bread Crumbs,
    United States, 329

COUNTRY-BY-COUNTRY INDEX
PAGE 331

1
BREAD
YESTERDAY AND TODAY

Bread A bun—small, round and soft to the touch; a loaf—large, dark and hard to break but yielding to a sharp knife. Think of the varieties of shape, texture, flavor. And the aroma. The fragrance of freshly-baked bread is universal and lingers in the memory like the smell of earth in spring or the tang of sea air.

We do not live by bread alone, but it has been our "staff of life" for centuries. Bread satisfies hunger—and much more. It is many things to many people.

Prehistoric man collected wild grains and ate them just as he found them. Then, in the fertile Nile Valley of Egypt, man stopped being a scavenger and turned to agriculture, the cultivation of the soil. Over the years, man experimented with the grains he grew: roasting them over fire, which removed the chaff and made them easier to digest; mixing them with water into a primitive porridge; making a thicker paste that could be formed into little cakes. At first these cakes were eaten raw, then baked on hot stones.

This unleavened bread, improved by the addition of shortening and salt, survives today in many countries. The Mexican tortilla, the Scots oatcake, the Indian chapati, the Chinese pao ping, as well as the American Indian johnnycake, are all variations of the original flatbread. And should you like to sample "bread in the raw," they're still serving it that way in Mongolia.

The discovery of leavened bread probably occurred by accident in the Nile Valley when some yeasty microorganism drifted into a mound of fresh dough and an eagle-eyed Egyptian gourmet noticed the rising phenomenon. Mesmerized, he may have watched it for hours until it stopped rising and then popped it into that recently-invented gadget—an oven. What emerged after baking was a lighter and tastier loaf than ever before. Word spread fast, and so did the variety of breads and cakes.

Capitalizing on the delicious discovery, Pharaoh soon had his keepers of the purse paying construction workers on the pyramids a daily wage of three loaves of bread and two jugs of beer. In those days, "bread" was "money" indeed!

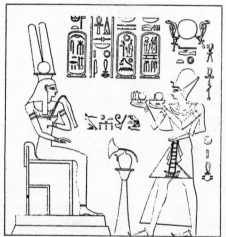

But there is an even richer tradition of bread as a major link in the life cycle, not just for sustenance, but as a symbol of fruitfulness and fertility. Thus, the concept of a female grain spirit exists in the folklore of many countries. In Denmark there's a rye woman; in Poland, a grandmother called Baba; and in Scotland, a fair maiden. Cherokee Indians have a ritual dance to "The Grandmother" of the corn. In ancient Greece, the goddess Demeter was skilled in the art of growing corn and she and her daughter, Persephone, were celebrated as symbols of the harvest and regeneration. Many well-wishers around the world still throw rice at the bride and groom, break bread over the bride's head, or put a piece of bread in her shoe to ensure a fruitful marriage.

In Sweden, loaves are fashioned in the shape of a female figure and eaten by the family to maintain health and fertility in the home. In fact, throughout Scandinavia the word bread is used to refer to a woman's breasts, especially if they are large. The entire breadmaking process —kneading, shaping and baking—is also a synonym for making love.

The creation of bread itself parallels and evokes the hidden, quiet growth of a child in the womb—hence the colloquialism "a bun in the oven" for pregnancy. In parts of Africa, the placenta of a newborn

baby used to be baked in ceremonial bread as a tribute to the generosity of the gods. One old Nordic custom dictated placing a morsel of bread in a newborn's mouth for a moment to bring it health, happiness and wealth. Another tradition entailed putting some bread in the baby's crib to ward off evil spirits. Throughout history, mortal man has used bread as a means of reaching out to immortal spirit. Among pagans, bread was often fashioned into animal shapes by the poor as a substitute offering to the gods. In Sweden, the extravagantly curlicued *Lussekatter,* yellow as the sun, originated as an effort to placate capricious deities. At the Last Supper, Christ imbued bread with a powerful symbolism and for nearly two thousand years a bread wafer has represented His body in the sacrament of Communion. Some other breads in the Christian tradition are hot-cross buns at Easter and pancakes on Shrove Tuesday.

The decorative braid of challah—the Jewish Sabbath bread—is said to symbolize a ladder to heaven, and the unleavened matzos of Passover are a reminder of the hasty Exodus from Egypt. The circular ring of Greek bread suggests a continuity of life. Moslems consider it sinful to slice bread with a knife—it must always be broken. All over the world people thank the Lord for their daily bread and ask Him to bless it. During the Middle Ages bread signified one's social standing. The wealthy demanded that their bread be "white" as an indication of their highly refined tastes. This in turn led some millers to mix anything from chalk dust or alum to ground ivory into their flour. Small wonder that they developed reputations as scoundrels and thieves. Remember Chaucer's miller in the Canterbury Tales? Even later in America, finding an honest miller was considered noteworthy, and so it was that Abraham Lincoln became known as "Honest Abe" when working as a youth in a small Illinois flour mill.

Although bakers had formed a guild in London by 1155, they too had their share of troubles. The citizens of each community were often obliged to supply their own dough to the local baker and, what's more, pay for the privilege. It was not too difficult for a nimble-fingered baker to appropriate portions of the dough for himself, leaving each customer's loaf a bit lighter, though not appreciably reduced in size. The "baker's dozen"—thirteen for the price of twelve—may have originated as a protection against shortweighting the consumer.

THE HARVEST-FIELD.

But who is protecting the consumer today from the cottonlike loaves labeled "bread" in the supermarkets? Many of these tasteless products are loaded with chemical additives and so lacking in natural vitamins and minerals that even mold refuses to grow on them. Why do we continue to buy this manufactured emptiness? Surely our tastebuds know better!

There is a natural alternative—become your own baker! You'll eat better, stay healthier, cut costs and calm your nerves in the bargain. What better punching bag than a plump wad of dough? Who can feel depressed participating in the magic of creating a delicious taste treat? It's a sensual, satisfying experience. Best of all, on occasion, the whole family can join in the fun and then share the "fruits" of their labor together, and with friends.

Breadbaking is not the difficult, time-consuming task of days gone by. Flours of great variety and texture, standardized measurements, and modern ovens provide an almost foolproof setting for beginner and expert alike. The most inexperienced baker need not have cold feet the first time around since it is almost impossible to create an unappetizing bread. Even a relative "flop" can be redeemed as bread crumbs, canapé bases, or bread pudding.

Today's baker has the advantage of many grains being available internationally and year round. Wheat, oat, rye, barley, rice, soy and

even peanut flours provide inspiration for original as well as traditional breads. Fruits, nuts, vegetables, natural sweeteners and cheese can be incorporated as tempting complements.

Take some time to visit church bazaars and fairs. There's a cornucopia of digestible delights awaiting you. And don't forget to check the family files for recipes you thought you'd never use.

I myself am from an international bread-loving family. There are few things I enjoy more than sharing homebaked bread, good wine and talk with friends. I have lived in many countries and have collected bread recipes the world over. My selections for this book were made with an eye towards ease in preparations, accessibility of ingredients, and, of course, the tastiest results. Throughout, I use the word "savory" as opposed to "sweet" to mean any bread that is not used as a coffee bread or other fancy bread.

All the recipes are nutritionally sound, easy to follow and require little or no previous baking experience. Each one has been tested several times and adjusted for the American kitchen when necessary. So let's roll up our sleeves, head for the kitchen and bake bread together!

2
INGREDIENTS
AND UTENSILS

Flours and grains There are many different kinds of flours and grains to use in baking. Here are some of the most common:

WHEAT FLOUR is what is usually meant by the term "flour." It is the most widely grown and used grain in the world: there are about 30,000 wheat varieties belonging to fourteen species. About 1,000 varieties are grown for commercial use and they belong to the class *triticum aestivum* which means common wheat.

Wheat's high gluten content makes it excellent for all kinds of baking, and wheat flour is usually added to breads made with other flours to improve their texture and consistency.

Wheat flour comes in two forms, bleached and unbleached. Both are used in the same way, but I prefer the unbleached because it is more wholesome yet lends itself to the most delicate breads, cakes and cookies. In fact, in Europe you can't even get bleached flour, but the breads and pastries they bake are wonderful. Fortunately, unbleached flour is available in American supermarkets.

Fig. 106. a Weizen. b Roggen. c Gerste. d Hafer

In Europe, you can buy special PASTRY FLOUR, which is a wheat flour of much softer quality. In this country, it is grown in the Midwest, but is virtually impossible to find in the supermarkets on the East coast. Therefore, I recommend regular unbleached flour when a recipe calls for pastry flour or just plain flour.

WHOLE-WHEAT FLOUR contains all the different parts of the wheat kernel, including the bran and the germ. Its appearance is somewhat coarse and gray and it makes a very nutritious and delicious bread. Try to get this flour stone-ground instead of steel-ground because the intense heat of modern steel mills destroys many important nutrients. This is equally true for other flours. Health food stores are a good source for a variety of stone-ground flours.

WHEAT GERM is the germ of the wheat kernel, the most nutritious part of the wheat. It is rich in vitamins B1, B2 and E as well as in protein and iron. The wheat germ is often removed from flour during the milling process. It has a delicious nutty flavor and there are many times when I smuggle a couple of spoonfuls of it into cake batter, in the belief that my children will be healthier as a result. Because of its high oil content wheat germ spoils quickly, so once a jar has been opened be sure to keep it in the refrigerator.

BRAN is part of whole-wheat flour, but can also be bought separately. Its cellulosic properties tend to speed food through the human digestive tract. In other words, it adds roughage to the diet and should be included in food for elderly or sedentary people.

All the above flours are types of wheat flour. BUCKWHEAT is altogether different. It comes from a plant grown in poor soil and is probably closer to corn than to any other grain. Buckwheat flour is used primarily for Russian and Scandinavian tiny *blinis* or *bovetepannkakor* or other Scandinavian breads. Add some to your dough; it will produce a heavy bread with a distinctive flavor.

RYE FLOUR also comes from a different plant. It is a darker flour with less gluten than wheat flour so it is advisable to mix some wheat flour with rye when you bake. Rye flour makes delicious bread and is very popular in Northern and Eastern Europe. It is rumored that rye bread eaters stay younger and live longer than wheat bread eaters, and judging by the longevity of some Eastern Europeans, this may be true.

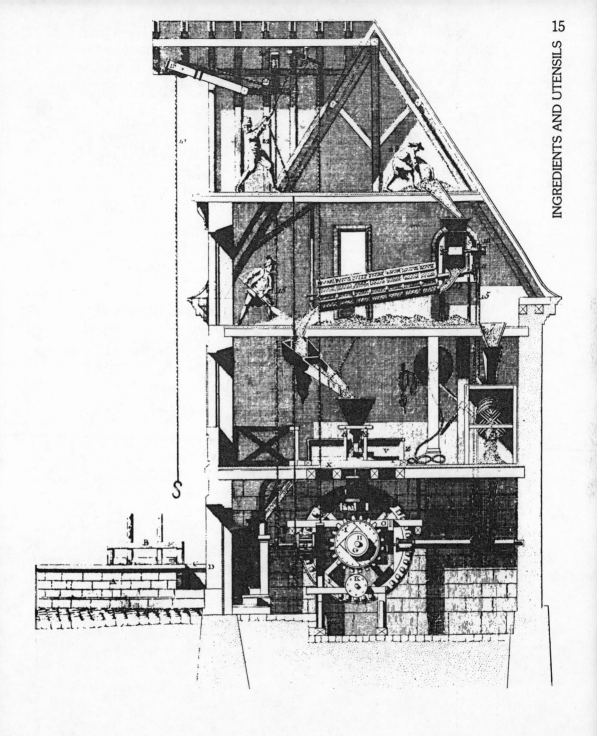

Rye grain is also used for making whiskey in the United States and, during hard times, roasted rye grain has been used as a coffee substitute.

RYE MEAL is rye flour of a coarse texture, but very tasty. Blend with some wheat flour for a full-flavored bread of finer texture.

BARLEY, together with wheat, was one of the first grains to be cultivated and widely grown in ancient Egypt. It is very flavorful and makes a versatile flour. Nowadays, one doesn't find many recipes calling for barley, but you may experiment by interchanging barley for whole-wheat or rye in your breads; or try it as a hot cereal or as an added treat in poultry stuffing.

CORN FLOUR, which the British call maize, comes from corn kernels. Corn flour, yellow or white, can be mixed with some wheat flour for satisfactory results when baking bread.

CORNMEAL is coarser and has a somewhat sweeter taste. It may be used in the same way as corn flour.

ROLLED OATS is a grain that has a rich, sweet taste and is great for mixing with wheat flour for a really tasty, nicely-textured bread. It is also used as a cereal and in baking certain cakes and cookies.

RICE FLOUR is actually ground rice, and when added to bread will give it a smooth, rather sweet flavor.

SOY FLOUR is an extremely nutritious flour, which I am sure will be getting a lot of attention in the future. It is rich in protein and contains all the amino acids that are important in the diet. You can use up to 25% soy flour in any bread you bake for a hearty, exceedingly nutritious bread. The same goes for SOY GRANULES which are somewhat coarser in texture and have a slightly nutty, or to some people, soapy taste.

PEANUT FLOUR is actually finely ground peanuts. Add some to your bread if you wish to provide extra protein. DRIED BEANS, CHICKPEAS and PEAS which have been ground into meal can also be used in bread baking.

Liquid is needed when making bread and WATER is of course the simplest and least expensive liquid you can use. But for some breads you can use MILK, either whole, skimmed, powdered, or evaporated.

BUTTERMILK and CREAM are sometimes used. You can also use water left over from boiling potatoes or other vegetables. BEER is used in baking, and so is leftover HOT CHOCOLATE or COFFEE, or even PEA or LENTIL SOUP. Just remember not to use too much of any liquid that has a distinctive taste, as it might noticeably alter the flavor of the bread. Basically, whenever the recipe calls for a diluting agent, water should be used.

I strive to use up leftovers imaginatively when I bake, to save money and be creative as well.

Leavenings To make your bread rise, to make it light and soft inside, you must use some kind of leavening. Not all breads, however, are supposed to rise and be soft, and for those you won't use any leavening at all.

The most common leavening for bread is YEAST, which comes in two forms: fresh, also called compressed; or dried, known as granulated. Fresh yeast is quite hard to come by and is rather perishable. I think it is superior to the dried (granulated) variety but I do use both kinds. If you can obtain fresh yeast, store it in the refrigerator and use it within two weeks. If it becomes dry and brown, discard it. Granulated yeast is widely available in supermarkets and you'll probably use it more frequently.

It comes in little foil envelopes, usually three attached together, each containing ¼ ounce. You can also find it in larger quantities in jars. Although every supermarket carries granulated yeast, for one reason or another they keep it well hidden. Look for the date on the package to make sure it's fresh; sometimes the fresh (compressed) yeast also carries a date. Granulated yeast is easy to work with, gives good results, and lasts for a long time. One envelope of granulated yeast contains about 1½ tablespoons and in use is equivalent to one ounce or half a cake of fresh yeast (almost all the fresh yeast comes in 2-ounce cakes).

For sourdough bread, you can easily make your own leavening. But, if you prefer, you can send for ready-made sourdough starters through magazine ads, or ask your local health food store to obtain it for you.

For other breads you'll be using BAKING POWDER or BAKING SODA. They are both simple to use and make for quick baking.

In some European countries they use a leavening called HARTSHORN SALT (actually ammonium carbonate). It can be obtained through a drugstore. Don't be surprised if your druggist looks at you strangely when you ask for it; it has been known to be used for witchcraft or love potions.

You may want to add some EGGS to your bread; go ahead, the more the merrier. Just remember to use proportionately less liquid. Eggs have a leavening effect and will make the bread light and lovely. Egg yolks alone will make white bread look rich and slightly yellow.

Shortenings

Sometimes you will want to add some kind of shortening to your bread for extra flavor and texture. There are many to choose from: BUTTER, MARGARINE, LARD, BACON FAT, PEANUT, CORN or other OILS; and in some instances, when the flavor is desired, OLIVE OIL. Butter and margarine are usually softened or melted and cooled in order to blend easily with the rest of the ingredients.

For deep frying such breads as doughnuts I prefer Crisco in the solid form.

Sweeteners

Often you'll be adding some kind of sweetener to your bread. The two most common sweeteners are PLAIN WHITE SUGAR and RAW BROWN SUGAR. A spoonful of sugar added to the yeast sponge makes it bubble more quickly. As for sweet coffee cakes, buns and rolls, the sweetener is added as a flavoring. You can achieve subtle flavor sensations by trying various kinds of HONEY when you bake. MOLASSES is often added to bread, but use it sparingly since it has a strong, bitter taste. CANE and MAPLE SYRUP give bread a special flavor and so does CAROB SYRUP. There are also assorted FRUIT SUGARS available at health food stores that might appeal to you.

Spices, etc. Spices, herbs and nuts can be added to your bread for flavorful variety: CUMIN, CARDAMOM and FENNEL are wonderful. Cardamom, in particular, gives coffee cakes a very clean, fresh taste. SAFFRON imparts intriguing flavor and a festive golden hue. SALT is also used in breadbaking, but in moderate amounts, since it inhibits the rising of the dough. I prefer kosher salt—it seems tastier to me. POMERANCE, which is really dried orange peel, is delicious in rye bread and in rusks. You may find it in specialty shops or you can make your own: cut an orange into 4 wedges and peel, removing the white membrane. Place the wedges of peel on foil in a 300-degree oven for 30 minutes or until the color is dark orange and the edges turn brown. Stored in a dry place with a tightly fitted lid, it will last indefinitely. It should be softened in a little boiling water and finely chopped before being added to dough. You must try PAPRIKA, PEPPER, CINNAMON, NUTMEG, CLOVES, ALLSPICE, GINGER, MACE, TURMERIC and CARAWAY SEEDS in your breads, too.

Fresh or dried herbs make interesting additions in bread or pancakes. Many different NUTS, chopped or ground, can be added to dough or batter, and while we're at it, don't forget RAISINS, CURRANTS, CRANBERRIES, SLICED APPLES, BLUEBERRIES, CHERRIES, CANDIED FRUITS and PEELS. Crisp crumbled BACON and grated CHEESE are great in some breads and so are ONIONS and GARLIC. On top of bread you can sprinkle POPPY SEED, SESAME SEED or COARSE SALT for both flavor and effect.

There is virtually no limit to what people all around the globe have been putting in their bread throughout history. The Swedes, during years of harsh famine, added up to 90 percent pine bark to their dough in order to stretch it for survival. Italian bakers mixed flour with the blood of horses during the Roman campaigns and in medieval France, oxblood was used in similar fashion. Scandinavians also bake a bread which contains, besides many spices, reindeer blood. Unappetizing? Perhaps. But think of the protein!

Above all in breadmaking, once you've mastered the fundamentals, let yourself go—have fun—experiment.

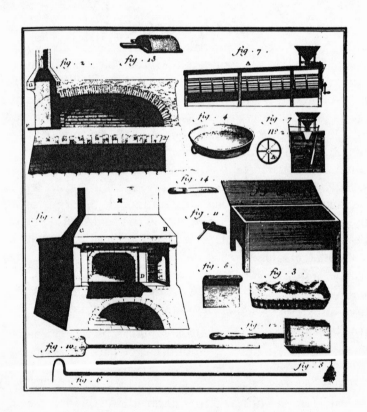

Utensils You don't need many special utensils in order to bake. With the simplest of tools you'll be able to produce delicious, fragrant and nutritious breads. You'll need:

A Bowl or Pot—for mixing the dough. If you don't have a large bowl, use a stockpot or washbasin or any vessel large enough to hold the dough during the mixing and rising, when it will double in size. Smaller mixing bowls are sufficient for batter-made breads.

A Sturdy Wooden Spoon

A Measuring Cup

A Set of Measuring Spoons

A Rolling Pin—the small ones you see in the supermarkets are not very good, so it is wise to invest in a really hefty one. In an emergency you can use an empty, smooth wine bottle.

A Pastry Brush—of good quality. I prefer the old-fashioned ones made from goose feathers. If you don't have one on hand, bunch together a piece of paper toweling and use that.

2 Kitchen Towels—or similar clean cloths to cover the dough while it rises. You can also use a sheet of plastic wrap, which will hasten the dough's rising because it is airtight.

A Working Surface—such as a kitchen table or a counter top, large enough for comfort when you knead the dough. The surface can be Formica or wood and should be kept spanking clean, as should your utensils.

Cookie Sheets—several

Loaf Pans—both round and oblong. These can be bought inexpensively at the five-and-ten. I prefer aluminum to glass.

Muffin Tins—a couple, holding a dozen each. I'm not mad for Teflon, but for muffin tins it's unsurpassed—so easy to clean, especially when buttered before baking.

A Cast-Iron Pan—for making pancakes.

An Electric Waffle Iron

Not necessary, but nice to have:

An Electric Mixer—for mixing and kneading dough with a special dough hook attachment. Most mixers are rather expensive, but if you plan to bake a lot, it's worthwhile acquiring a good one if you can. It saves time and effort in the kitchen.

A Dough Mixer—a less expensive device to use for kneading. It must be cranked by hand but still cuts down on kneading time.

A Special Apron—just for baking

A Kerchief—for your hair. It looks attractive and, besides, nobody likes hairy bread.

Naturally, if you want, you can spend a great deal of money on terrific gadgets, beautiful baking pans, fancy stainless steel bowls and more. However, the most important tool is your own two hands. And the most important asset is a heart full of love for the work you do, and for those who will enjoy your delectable creations.

3
TIPS ON BAKING

Starting Occasionally the amount of flour and the baking times in this book may not be as precise as they are in general cookbooks. But in bread baking, many factors determine the amount of flour to use: the type of flour, the commercial brand, how it is packed in the measuring cup, and how precisely everything else is measured. It is always best not to add all the flour at once when baking with yeast. You can always add some more flour if the dough seems too loose and sticky.

As for baking time, that depends on the accuracy of your oven, the length of time the oven door is kept open, and the dampness or dryness of the weather. You must also consider personal taste preferences. Some enjoy a light-colored crust on their bread, while others prefer it dark or almost burned. You have to use your judgment when baking and, of course, the experience gained after several baking sessions will be most helpful.

The first step in baking is to check that you have on hand all the ingredients needed for your recipe. Take them out and let them reach room temperature if they are cold. If you keep the flour in the refrigerator, take it out the night before baking so that it will reach room temperature by the time you are ready to use it.

Try to keep the kitchen at approximately 75 degrees when you bake, or even warmer, and close any windows. The dough doesn't like a cold and drafty kitchen.

Then, wash and scrub your hands, put on a large, clean apron, and, if your hair is long, cover it with a kerchief.

When you bake in the hot summer months, start early in the morning. Baking in 95 degree weather is no picnic, and it can easily get that hot in the kitchen with the oven on all day.

Now that the preliminaries are completed, down to the actual work! First we have to "proof" the yeast, especially if it is the fresh (compressed) variety. I like to proof the dry granulated yeast as well because I feel it enhances the bread's flavor.

To proof the yeast means testing to see if it is alive, and I mean *alive!* Yeast is a living organism which, when activated, releases a gas making bread rise and get soft. If the yeast is too old it may be dead and will not promote rising. The envelopes of dry granulated yeast are dated for freshness so, if you're using them, proofing is not always necessary. In some recipes it is required and in others it isn't, so always follow the recipe at hand.

Here's the basic method for proofing:
In a large bowl, pour some liquid, approximately ¼ cup of liquid per envelope of granulated or ounce of fresh yeast. The liquid can be water, milk, potato water or whatever you are using to bake with, and the temperature should be about 95 degrees for fresh yeast and up to 115 degrees for granulated yeast. If the liquid is too warm it will kill the yeast spores; if it is too cold, it will bubble and rise eventually but it will take a long time.

In the beginning I would advise you to use a thermometer; as you become a more experienced baker you will be able to judge the temperature just by touching the liquid.

Crumble the fresh yeast or sprinkle the granulated yeast into the liquid. To hasten bubbling, add a little sugar, about one teaspoon is enough. No salt though, since that inhibits the fermenting process.

Now cover the bowl with a towel or for faster results, a plastic sheet, and place in a warm, draft-free place. If conditions are good, the yeast should start to bubble and rise in 10 to 15 minutes. If this does not happen within 30 minutes I suggest you throw the yeast mixture out and start anew.

When the yeast is activated, resulting in a "yeast sponge," you can add the rest of the liquid, lukewarm of course, then the melted butter, eggs and sugar or whatever the recipe calls for, and finally the flour, but not all of it at the same time. Leave about one quarter of the flour aside to be used for kneading the dough on the work surface. As I mentioned earlier, if there is not enough flour in the dough you can always add some more, but if you have added too much, it is impossible to remove it.

The blending—mixing the ingredients together—comes next, and is followed by the kneading of the dough. For blending use a wooden spoon, a dough mixer or an electric mixer with a dough hook attachment. Mix until all the ingredients hold together and form a dough that is shiny and does not adhere to the sides of the bowl. Now turn the dough out onto a floured work surface and knead it with your hands. If the dough seems too soft and sticky, add more flour and knead it until it is shiny and has a good elastic feel. When it reaches this stage, stop. Don't overknead the dough.

When you are finished kneading the dough, place it in a large oiled or buttered bowl, roll the dough around to coat it with the fat, sprinkle a little flour on top and cover with a towel, or for speedier rising, a plastic sheet.

Place the bowl in a warm, draft-free place and allow the dough to rise until double in size. (Some bakers use their unlit oven for the first rising.) This takes approximately 1 hour, but the time may vary slightly, so follow the instructions in each recipe.

After the first rising, turn the dough out again onto your lightly floured work surface, punch it down a few times and knead some more. Now put it back in the bowl to rise again, or shape your loaves or buns and place them in their baking pans or baking sheets covered or uncovered, according to the instructions in the recipe. In either case, let the dough or shaped breads rise for another half hour to forty minutes. Meanwhile, light your oven.

If the recipe calls for brushing the tops of the loaves with butter or eggs or anything else, do so before placing the breads in the oven. Some breads, however, are brushed after they are baked.

Now place your breads in the oven and bake until they reach the desired color. If the breads seem to brown too quickly, cover them with a piece of foil. When done, they should feel hollow when you tap them with your finger and they should shrink from the sides of the pan (if you are using a pan).

Place your baked bread on a rack to cool. If you like a soft crust, cover the cooling bread with a towel. If you prefer a hard crust, leave it uncovered.

Treat yourself and taste some of the bread while it is still warm; what a pleasure!

After your breads are thoroughly cooled, wrap them in plastic bags. Homebaked bread lasts much longer in the bread box than the supermarket kind. However, if you freeze your bread, you must use it rather quickly once it has been thawed.

Once a week I like to bake our family's staple bread, which is six loaves of white bread and six loaves of dark bread. I freeze three of each kind and leave the rest in the bread box. During the week whenever I feel like baking something special I'll bake again, but I always bake our most popular breads once a week.

4
WHAT WENT WRONG

Results As with everything else, things do go wrong occasionally when you bake, but it is rarely a hopeless situation. There is almost no such thing as a really bad loaf of homebaked bread, and at worst, you can always make bread crumbs from the bread. Here are some of the most common mistakes to occur in baking:

The dough will not rise
This is probably the worst thing that will happen, and your best bet is to start all over again. Some of the reasons for dough not rising are:

The yeast was too old. (Always check the expiration date on the dry yeast packages. With fresh yeast, make sure that it is not dried and brown.)

Your liquid was too warm. The ideal temperature for the liquid in which you dissolve or proof the packaged, granulated yeast is from 105 to 115 degrees, and for the fresh (compressed) yeast, 95 degrees.

The flour was too cold. If you keep your flour in a cold place make sure to take it out in time to reach room temperature before you start to bake.

You put the dough in a place that was too cold or too drafty for it to rise.

The last, but probably least likely reason, is that you worked the dough too long.

The finished bread is too hard
This is a common occurrence among beginning bakers, but nothing to worry about. With more practice your bread will improve.

Too much flour in the dough is the usual reason for hard bread.

Too much sugar could also be the cause, or perhaps you did not let the bread rise long enough after it was shaped.

But you can still enjoy the hard bread. Just slice it very thinly and spread with lots of butter. Or, use the thin bread slices as a base for canapés and pretend that it was supposed to be this way.

The bread seems too heavy
The most common reasons are:

Too much shortening or sugar.

You didn't let the bread rise long enough after it was shaped. Use the bread the same way as indicated above.

The bread has a layer of unbaked dough
In German, this mishap is described by a very special tongue-twisting word which I love: *Sitzengeblieben* (was left sitting). The reasons might be:

Your oven was not hot enough.

You may have put too much sugar into the dough.

It didn't rise long enough after you shaped it.

Don't throw the bread away; just cut off the unbaked part and use the bread as a base for canapés. You can cut off the crust, too, and use it for crumbs.

The bread has cracks on top of the crust
Not a very serious problem, but the reasons might be:

You did not mix the dough enough.

The bread contains too much flour.

You didn't let the bread rise long enough after it was shaped.

The bread crumbles and the texture is coarse
This is a very common problem with beginning bakers and the reason is almost always:

The baker lets the dough rise too long after it is shaped.

The last rising of the dough, when the bread is shaped, is the most critical. Don't let the dough stand too long to rise after you have shaped it. Even with the coarse texture the bread will taste good, but it will be difficult to slice. Either eat it by breaking off into pieces or make bread crumbs out of it.

The bread has large air bubbles
　　Most likely the dough was poorly mixed.
　　The dough rose too much.
　　The dough was kept in a place that was too warm after it was shaped.

Here are some common mistakes that occur when baking with other leavening, such as baking powder and baking soda.

The bread cracks
The reasons for this could be:
　　The oven was too hot.
　　You didn't blend the flour and leavening thoroughly.

The bread rises over the brim of the baking pan
　　Your baking pan is too small.
　　You used too much leavening.
　　The oven was not hot enough.

The bread won't rise
The usual reason for this is that the bread did not have a chance to finish baking, or perhaps you opened the oven door prematurely or tested the bread too early with a skewer. (Some recipes call for this testing procedure but be sure to wait until you think the bread is done.)
　　The batter could have been stirred too much after the addition of the flour and leavening.

The bread doesn't rise evenly
　　The batter was not mixed enough.

5
SAVORY BREADS
WITH YEAST

PEDA BREAD

You will get two fragrant puffed breads from this recipe. Serve warm or cold. They are delicious split and filled with a sandwich spread.

Yield: 2 round 8" breads. Can be frozen.

1 envelope yeast
¼ cup lukewarm water
2 Tbs. sugar
1 cup water
3 Tbs. lard
1 Tbs. salt

4 cups flour
Warm water to brush the
  tops
4 Tbs. sesame seeds
  (approximately)

Preheat the oven to 400 degrees.

Proof the yeast in the lukewarm water with the sugar.

Place the 1 cup of water in a saucepan with the lard and bring to a boil. Remove from the heat and cool to lukewarm.

Blend the yeast sponge with the water and lard mixture, stir in the salt and flour.

Now place the dough on a lightly floured work surface and knead until shiny and smooth. Place the dough in a large buttered bowl, cover with a towel and let rise in a warm place for about 1 hour or until doubled in bulk.

Take the dough out and knead it again for about 1 minute. Put the dough back into the bowl and let stand for 20 minutes, covered with a towel.

Again place the dough on the work surface and knead for a couple of minutes. Divide into 2 equal pieces, and with your hands, shape into 2 round cakes, about ½" to ¾" thick and place on a buttered baking sheet. Cover with a towel and let stand in a warm place for about 30 minutes or until doubled in size.

Brush with the warm water and sprinkle the sesame seeds on top to taste.

Bake until light brown and puffed—this should take about 25 to 30 minutes. Cool on rack.

KARTOFFELBROT
Potato Bread

Kartoffelbrot was baked and eaten in my husband's home in Vienna. I still make it the way his grandmother did.

We love it, plain or toasted with butter—either way it is a good bread.

Yield: 2 large loaves. Can be frozen.

1 envelope yeast	¼ cup honey
½ cup lukewarm water	1 Tbs. salt
2 Tbs. sugar	½ cup milk, scalded and
1½ cups flour	cooled to lukewarm
1 egg yolk	Grated rind of 1 lemon
3 Tbs. soft butter	3 to 4 cups flour
½ cup cooked, mashed	1 cup sultana raisins
potatoes	

Preheat the oven to 400 degrees.

Proof the yeast in the lukewarm water with the sugar. Add the 1½ cups of flour and the egg yolk to the yeast sponge; stir well and set aside in a warm place, covered with a towel. Let rise until doubled in bulk.

Now add the soft butter, mashed potatoes, honey, salt, milk and lemon rind. Stir well. Add the flour, a little at a time, stirring until you have a smooth dough. Add the sultana raisins and place the dough on a lightly floured work surface. Knead the dough until it is shiny and doesn't stick to your hands. Add some flour if necessary.

Place the dough in a large buttered bowl, cover with a towel and let stand in a warm place to rise for about 1 hour or until doubled in bulk.

Take the dough, punch it down a couple of times, divide into 2 equal pieces, knead and shape these into loaves and place in 2 large (9″ by 5″) buttered loaf pans.

Cover with a towel and let rise until doubled in bulk.

Bake in the oven until golden brown and the loaves sound hollow when tapped with your finger, about 40 to 45 minutes.

Cool for a couple of minutes in the pans, then remove from the pans and continue to cool with the loaves wrapped in a towel.

NEW BRUNSWICK OATMEAL BREAD

Make sandwiches out of this bread for your children's lunch boxes. The bread is soft and spongy, which children like, and it is far more wholesome than the white supermarket bread.

Yield: 3 large loaves. Can be frozen.

2 envelopes yeast
½ cup lukewarm water
3 tsps. sugar
2½ cups boiling water
1½ cups oatmeal
1 cup scalded milk

1 stick butter
2 Tbs. salt
¾ cup molasses
2 cups whole-wheat flour
6 to 7 cups all-purpose flour

Preheat the oven to 450 degrees.

Proof the yeast in the ½ cup lukewarm water with the sugar.

Pour the boiling water into a bowl with the oatmeal and stir.

Add the stick of butter to the scalded milk. When it is melted pour it into the bowl containing the oatmeal and water. Add the salt and molasses, stir and let the mixture stand until lukewarm.

Now add the lukewarm oatmeal mixture to the yeast sponge, stir in the whole-wheat flour and add the all-purpose flour, 1 cup at a time, stirring after each addition. When it is firm enough to handle, place the dough on a lightly floured work surface and knead until shiny, adding more flour if it is sticky.

Place the dough in a large buttered bowl, cover with a towel and let it rise in a warm, draft-free place until it is doubled in bulk. This should take about 1 hour.

When the dough has risen, punch it down a couple of times and divide it into 3 equal pieces. Place these pieces into 3 large buttered loaf pans (9" by 5"), cover and let rise for about 45 minutes, or until the loaves are doubled in size.

Bake in the 450-degree oven for 15 minutes, then reduce the heat to 375 degrees and continue to bake for about another 20 minutes or until the loaves are nicely brown on top.

Remove the breads from the oven and let them cool in the pans for about 10 minutes. Then remove the loaves, wrap them in a towel and let them cool completely.

HUA CHUAN
Rolls

These are Chinese rolls that you can serve with your own home-cooked Chinese dinner. They are plain and go with many different dishes. For a different flavor, you may like to substitute roasted sesame seeds for the salt.

Yield: About 16 rolls. Do not freeze.

1 envelope yeast
1½ cups lukewarm water
1 heaping Tbs. light brown
   sugar
1 Tbs. vegetable oil (not
   olive oil)

3 cups flour
Dash of salt
¼ cup vegetable oil (not
   olive oil)
Some salt or sesame seeds

Proof the yeast in the lukewarm water with the sugar.

Stir in the 1Tbs. oil, the flour, and salt and blend well.

Turn out onto a lightly floured work surface and knead until shiny and smooth.

Place the dough in a large oiled bowl, cover with a towel and let stand in a warm place to rise until doubled in bulk. This should take about 1 hour.

Now take the dough out, knead it again and divide into 3 pieces. With a rolling pin roll each piece into a very thin rectangle, as thin as you can without breaking the dough.

Brush the dough with the ¼ cup vegetable oil, sprinkle the salt on top and roll up, jelly-roll fashion.

Cut into 2″ slices. With a chopstick or the blunt edge of a knife press down the middle of each slice so that the edges stand up slightly and the roll resembles a butterfly.

Steam the rolls, a few at a time, in a bamboo or metal steamer for about 30 minutes or until cooked through.

PAN DE CUBA DE AFUERA DURA
Crusty Bread from Cuba

A good crusty bread that is delicious just plain with a glass of wine and perhaps some cheese.

Yield: 2 loaves. Can be frozen.

1 envelope yeast	6 to 7 cups flour
2 cups lukewarm water	2 Tbs. salt
1 Tbs. sugar	2 to 3 Tbs. corn flour

Do not preheat the oven this time!

Proof the yeast in the lukewarm water with the sugar in a large mixing bowl.

Add the flour and the salt, a little at a time, stirring and mixing until you have a rather stiff dough. Remove to a lightly floured work surface and knead the dough for a few minutes, then place it in a large buttered bowl, cover with a towel and let it rise in a warm place for about 1 hour or until it has doubled in bulk.

Again, remove the dough to the floured work surface and punch it down a couple of times. Divide into 2 equal pieces and shape into 2 oblong loaves about 18" long.

Sprinkle a baking sheet with the corn flour and place the loaves on top. Cover and let rise for a few minutes.

Now place the baking sheet with the 2 loaves on the upper rack in your oven. On the rack beneath the baking sheet place a tin form with hot water and turn the oven on to 400 degrees.

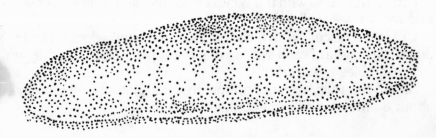

Bake the breads for about 16 minutes or until a crust begins to form. Remove from the oven and brush the tops with cold water, then return the breads to the oven and bake about 30 minutes more, or until they are golden.

Cool on a rack.

KARTOFFELBRØD
Potato Bread

A white bread with a wonderful texture and flavor. Great for sandwiches.

Yield: 2 large loaves. Can be frozen.

1 envelope yeast
½ cup lukewarm potato water (water in which you have boiled potatoes)
4 Tbs. sugar
1 stick soft butter
3 eggs

2 tsps. salt
1 cup cooked, mashed potatoes
1 cup milk
6 to 7 cups flour
2 Tbs. melted butter for brushing the tops

Preheat the oven to 375 degrees.

Proof the yeast in the lukewarm potato water with the sugar.

Cream the butter and add the eggs, 1 at a time, beating the mixture well. Add the salt, the mashed potatoes and the yeast sponge. Stir in the milk and add the flour, cup by cup, until you have a dough that is stiff enough to knead.

Remove the dough to a lightly floured work surface and knead until shiny.

Place the dough in a large buttered bowl, cover with a towel and let rise for about 45 minutes or until doubled in bulk.

Remove the dough and place on the work surface, kneading again for a few minutes.

Divide into 2 equal pieces, shape and place each into a large loaf pan (9" by 5"). Cover with a towel and let rise until doubled in size.

Just before you put them in the oven, brush the tops with the melted butter.

Bake approximately 35 to 40 minutes or until the loaves are golden brown and sound hollow when tapped with your finger.

Cool wrapped in a towel.

SOUR BREAD

Would you like to bake something that tastes like a sourdough bread, without the trials of making a starter? Try this. Perfect to slice and eat with butter and cold cuts.

Yield: 2 large loaves. Can be frozen.

1 envelope yeast	1 tsp. salt
2 cups lukewarm water	1 Tbs. caraway seeds
3½ cups rye flour	2 Tbs. melted butter for
1 cup all-purpose flour	brushing the tops

Preheat the oven to 375 degrees.

The night before you bake make the yeast sponge, which will first rise and then fall, turning sour by the next day.

Dissolve the yeast in the 2 cups of lukewarm water, and with a spoon stir in 2 cups of the rye flour, mixing until well blended.

Cover the sponge with a sheet of plastic and put it in a warm, draft-free place until the next day.

The next day the sponge will smell slightly sour. Now add 1 more cup of rye flour, the all-purpose flour, salt and caraway seeds.

Work the ingredients together until everything is well blended. Place the dough in a large buttered bowl, cover and let rise in a warm place for 1 hour or until doubled in bulk.

Turn the dough out onto the work surface which you have already sprinkled with the remaining ½ cup of rye flour. Knead and work the dough until it is smooth.

Divide into 2 pieces, shape and place in 2 buttered loaf pans (9″ by 5″). Cover the breads with a towel and let them rise again in a warm place for 1 hour.

Bake the loaves in the oven on the uppermost rack for approximately 1 hour.

Remove from the oven and, while still warm, brush the golden tops with the melted butter. Let the breads cool slightly, then remove them from the pans and continue to let cool, wrapped in a towel.

BARLEY BREAD

It is said that the pyramids were built with bread and onions. Perhaps a bread like this one gave the workers the strength and stamina to build those awesome monuments to their Pharaohs.

This recipe is for only one loaf of bread. Once you've tried it, you may want to increase the ingredients proportionately to get two or more breads.

Yield: 1 small round bread. Can be frozen.

1 envelope yeast	1 egg, slightly beaten
½ cup lukewarm water	2 Tbs. shortening
2 Tbs. honey	2 cups barley flour
½ tsp. salt	

Preheat the oven to 425 degrees.

Proof the yeast in the lukewarm water with the honey.

Add the salt, egg and shortening. Stir in the flour and blend until you have a dough that you can knead. Knead for a couple of minutes on a lightly floured work surface.

Place the dough in a large greased bowl, cover with a towel and let stand in a warm place for 1½ hours. The dough will not double in bulk, but will rise slightly.

Turn the dough out on a lightly floured work surface; knead again and shape until you have a round cake, about ½" thick. Place on a lightly greased baking sheet, cover with a towel and let stand for 1 hour.

Bake 15 to 20 minutes or until pale brown and the bread sounds hollow when tapped.

Cool on a rack.

WHEAT BREAD

After much research, I believe that this recipe is as close as one can come to duplicating the first leavened bread baked in ancient Egypt. Use unbleached flour.

By the way, the bread tastes very good when broken into pieces and eaten plain, or slit and filled with a sandwich filling.

Yield: 6 small loaves. Can be frozen.

1 envelope yeast
1½ cups lukewarm water
1 Tbs. honey

1 tsp. salt
Almost 4 cups flour

Preheat the oven to 425 degrees.

Proof the yeast in the lukewarm water with the honey. Stir in the salt and the flour, a little at a time until you have a rather stiff dough. Knead a couple of times on a lightly floured work surface, then place in a large greased bowl, cover with a towel and let rise for about 1 hour or until doubled in bulk.

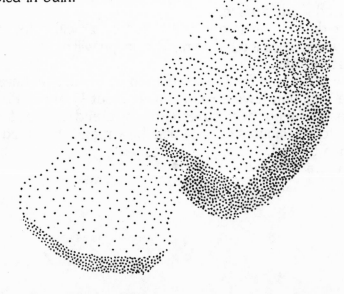

Take the dough and knead it again for a couple of minutes and divide into 6 equal pieces.

Knead and shape these pieces into ovals about ¼" thick and place on a greased baking sheet. Cover with a towel and let stand in a warm place to rise until doubled in size. This should take about ½ hour.

Before baking, poke a few random holes in the dough with a wooden or bamboo skewer.

Bake until light brown, about 15 to 20 minutes. Serve warm or cold. Cool on a rack.

BREADS OF THE WORLD

GRAHAM SQUARES

Serve these warm for breakfast or use cold as a sandwich base.

Yield: 8 square buns. Can be frozen.

1 envelope yeast
1½ cups lukewarm water
1 tsp. salt
2 cups whole-wheat flour
⅓ cup wheat germ

1½ to 2 cups all-purpose
    flour
2 Tbs. wheat germ to
    sprinkle on top

Preheat the oven to 400 degrees.

Dissolve the yeast in the lukewarm water. Stir in the salt, the whole-wheat flour and the wheat germ. Add the all-purpose flour, about ½ cup at a time.

Blend until you have a smooth dough that is not sticky. Place the dough on a lightly floured work surface and knead for about 5 minutes until the dough is very smooth and shiny.

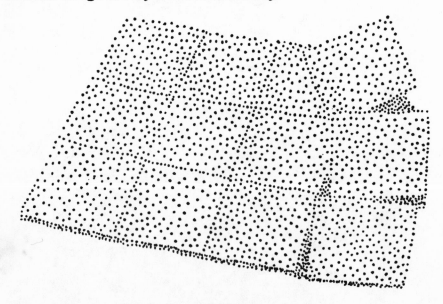

Place the dough in a large buttered bowl, cover with a towel and let rise for about 45 minutes.

Take the dough and knead it for a couple of minutes; flatten into a rectangle and place in a rectangular baking pan (11″ by 7″) that has been well buttered.

With a pastry wheel cut the dough into 8 squares. Cut right through the dough.

Cover with a towel and place in a warm place to rise for about ½ hour or until doubled in size.

Bake until golden brown for approximately 20-25 minutes.

Break off the squares and enjoy hot with butter. Or let cool in pan.

HONEY BREAD

Serve this warm or cold, spread with butter and honey.

Yield: 1 large bread. Can be frozen.

1 envelope yeast	2 Tbs. ground coriander
¼ cup lukewarm water	1 tsp. ground cinnamon
¾ stick butter, melted	½ tsp. ground cloves
1 cup milk	1 tsp. salt
½ cup honey	4 to 5 cups flour

Preheat the oven to 350 degrees.

Dissolve the yeast in the lukewarm water.

Melt the butter in a saucepan, and when it is all melted pour in the milk.

Add the honey, the butter-and-milk mixture, coriander, cinnamon, cloves and salt to the yeast mixture. Stir in the flour, 1 cup at a time, mixing until you have a dough that you can knead on your work surface. Knead for a few minutes. Add more flour if the dough is sticky. The dough should not be stiff, but rather loose.

Place the dough in a large buttered bowl, cover and put in a warm place to rise for about 1 hour or until it is doubled in bulk.

Now turn the dough out onto your lightly floured work surface, punch it down a couple of times, and place it in a 3-quart round pyrex or soufflé dish.

Cover and let rise again for about 45 minutes.

Bake in the oven, making sure you have plenty of room on top because this beautiful bread will rise like a soufflé.

Bake for about 40 minutes or until golden and the bread sounds hollow when tapped with your finger.

Remove from the baking pan after 5 minutes, then continue to cool on a rack.

BUCKWHEAT BREAD

Perhaps you like the inimitable flavor of buckwheat as much as I do. If so, you must try this bread which has a fine consistency that makes it easy to cut for sandwiches.

This bread goes particularly well with butter and a strong-tasting cheese, such as a Scandinavian spice cheese or American Sharp Cheddar.

Yield: 1 large loaf. Can be frozen.

1 envelope yeast
2 cups lukewarm water
1 Tbs. light brown sugar
¾ cup buttermilk
1 tsp. salt

2 eggs, slightly beaten
2 cups buckwheat flour
2 cups whole-wheat flour
About 1 cup all-purpose flour
1 Tbs. caraway seeds

Preheat the oven to 400 degrees.

Proof the yeast in the lukewarm water with the sugar.

After you get a yeast sponge add the buttermilk (room temperature), salt, eggs and the three different kinds of flour and caraway seeds. Mix well.

Take the dough out onto a lightly floured work surface, kneading until smooth.

Place the dough in a large buttered bowl, cover with a towel and let stand in a warm place to rise until doubled in bulk. This will take from 1½ to 2 hours.

Take the dough out and punch it down a couple of times. Knead and shape the dough into a loaf and place in a buttered loaf pan (9″ by 5″). Let stand in a warm place, covered with a towel, to rise for about 1 hour or until doubled in size.

Brush the bread with a little melted butter and bake in the oven for about 30 minutes or until light brown and the bread sounds hollow when tapped with your finger.

Cool wrapped in a towel.

FINNISH RYE BREAD

Slice into generous pieces and spread with butter and thick slices of cheese. That's the kind of bread this is!

Yield: 2 small loaves. Can be frozen.

1 envelope yeast
¼ cup lukewarm water
½ cup molasses
1½ cups buttermilk
1 Tbs. salt

1 Tbs. caraway seeds
Grated rind of 1 orange
3 cups rye flour
2 cups all-purpose flour

Preheat the oven to 375 degrees.

Dissolve the yeast in the lukewarm water.

In a saucepan bring the molasses to a boil, turn off the heat, measure in the buttermilk and stir until well blended.

When cooled to lukewarm add to the yeast mixture. Stir in the salt, caraway seeds and grated orange rind. Add the rye flour and about 1½ cups of the all-purpose flour and blend well.

Transfer the dough to a work surface that has been sprinkled with the rest of the all-purpose flour and knead until smooth and elastic. Add some more all-purpose flour if the dough sticks.

Place the dough in a large buttered bowl, cover with a towel and let stand in a warm place to rise for about 1 hour or until doubled in bulk.

Punch the dough down a couple of times and divide into 2 equal pieces. Knead and shape these into loaves and put into 2 small (8″ by 4″) loaf pans.

Cover with a towel and let rise until doubled in size, about 45 minutes.

Bake in the oven until brown on top and the loaves sound hollow when tapped with your finger. This should take approximately 30 to 35 minutes.

Cool for about 10 minutes in the pans, then remove the loaves and continue to cool them wrapped in a towel.

FRENCH BREAD

After much experimenting, this recipe is the closest I have ever come to imitating the fabulous French loaves.

The outside is crusty and the inside is just right. If you want an even crustier bread, place a pan with hot water in the oven on the next rack down from the baking sheet.

You can brush the breads with milk, egg yolks, egg white or leave them unbrushed. I usually use a beaten egg white, which makes a delightful shiny crust. Use unbleached flour and fresh (compressed) yeast if you can get it.

Yield: 3 small loaves. Can be frozen.

1 cake fresh yeast (2 oz.) or
   2 envelopes dry yeast
2 cups lukewarm water
1 tsp. sugar
1 Tbs. salt
5½ to 6 cups unbleached
   flour

1 beaten egg white to brush
   the loaves
A couple of Tbs. of cornmeal
   to sprinkle on the
   baking sheets

Preheat the oven to 450 degrees.

Crumble the yeast in the lukewarm water and add the sugar. Cover and let it turn into a sponge. Add the salt and the flour, cup by cup.

When you have a rather stiff dough, turn it out onto a lightly floured work surface and knead until well blended and not sticky. Add some more flour if necessary.

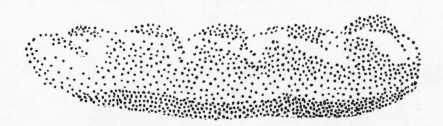

Place the dough in a large buttered bowl, cover with a towel and put in a warm place to rise for several hours. I sometimes let the dough stand for 3 to 5 hours, because I feel that this bread tastes better if allowed to rise for a long time on the first rising. You can completely forget about it; it needs no special attention, only a large bowl in which to rise.

After the dough has risen turn it out onto your floured work surface, punch it down and knead until shiny. Then divide into 3 equal pieces.

With the help of a rolling pin, roll each piece out into a rectangle, about 2 inches shorter than your baking sheet and 5 to 6 inches wide. Roll the dough up tightly as you would a jelly roll and place on the baking sheet, which has been sprinkled with the cornmeal.

Put in a warm place, cover with a towel and let rise for about 20 minutes. With a razor blade cut about 5 slashes diagonally in each loaf, brush with the beaten egg white and place in the hot oven.

Bake about 30 to 35 minutes or until golden and the loaves sound hollow when tapped with your finger. Serve hot or cold. Use for sandwiches, eat plain or turn into garlic bread (see page 328).

Cool on a rack.

FRENCH COUNTRY RYE BREAD

The dough for this good rye bread is a sort of sourdough, but it is easy to make. You must, however, start the yeast the day before you are going to bake.

Yield: 2 large loaves. Can be frozen.

For the starter you'll need:
- 1 envelope yeast
- 1¼ cups lukewarm water
- 1 Tbs. cider vinegar
- 1¼ cups all-purpose flour

The next day you add the following:
- 2 cups lukewarm water
- 1 Tbs. salt
- 1 Tbs. vegetable oil (not olive oil)
- 6 cups coarse rye flour (rye meal)
- 2 cups all-purpose flour
- A couple of Tbs. cornmeal to sprinkle on baking sheets

The day before you bake, dissolve the yeast in the 1¼ cups of lukewarm water. Add the cider vinegar and stir in the 1¼ cups of all-purpose flour, stirring until well blended.

Cover tightly with a sheet of plastic and let stand overnight in a warm place.

The next day:

Preheat the oven to 400 degrees.

To the yeast mixture, that will now have a slightly sourish odor, add the 2 cups of lukewarm water, salt, vegetable oil and rye flour. Add the all-purpose flour, a little at a time, until you have a dough that you can knead.

Place the dough on a lightly floured work surface and knead until it is shiny and not sticky anymore.

Place the dough in a large buttered bowl, cover with a towel and let stand in a warm place for about 1 to 2 hours or until the dough has doubled in bulk.

Place the dough on the work surface and knead for a couple of minutes. Divide into 2 equal pieces, continue to knead and shape into 2 long loaves, 2 inches shorter than your baking sheet.

Place these side by side on a baking sheet that has been sprinkled with cornmeal, and cut rather deep slits diagonally across the tops with a razor blade.

Cover with a towel and let stand in a warm place for about 1 hour or until the 2 loaves have doubled in bulk.

Bake in the oven for about 30 minutes or until they are light brown and sound hollow when tapped with your finger.

Cool on a rack.

GANNAT
Cheese Bread

A very good cheese bread that you can either toast or eat as is. It really should be made with Emmenthaler or Gruyère cheese, but many times I have used sharp Cheddar cheese as a substitute.

Yield: 2 large round loaves. Can be frozen.

1 envelope yeast
¼ cup lukewarm water
1 tsp. sugar
2 sticks soft butter
8 eggs

1 tsp. salt
4 to 5 cups flour
1½ cups grated cheese:
　　Emmenthaler, Gruyère
　　(Swiss), or Cheddar

Preheat the oven to 400 degrees.

Proof the yeast in the water with the sugar.

Cream the butter and stir in the eggs, 1 at a time, and the salt. Use an electric mixer for this, if you have one.

Add the flour, enough for a dough that is not too soft, but stiff enough to knead. Stir in the grated cheese.

Knead the dough on a lightly floured work surface for a few minutes and then place in a large buttered bowl, cover with a towel and let stand in a warm place to rise for 1 to 1½ hours.

Take the dough out again and knead for several minutes. Divide into 2 equal pieces. Shape these into round loaves and place them in 2 round cake forms (9") that have been buttered. Cover with a towel and let stand in a warm place to rise until doubled in size, about 1 hour.

Bake for about 30 minutes or until nicely brown and the breads sound hollow when tapped with your finger.

Cool on a rack.

WALNUT BREAD FROM BURGUNDY

A glass of port wine, a dish of fresh walnuts and some of this bread, still warm, make a fine afternoon snack.

Yield: 4 small round loaves. Can be frozen.

1 envelope yeast
½ cup lukewarm milk
1 tsp. sugar
1 stick butter
1½ cups milk

1 tsp. salt
5 to 6 cups flour
¾ cup minced onions
1 cup chopped walnuts

Preheat the oven to 400 degrees.

Proof the yeast in the ½ cup lukewarm milk with the sugar.

Melt the stick of butter, then stir the 1½ cups milk into the melted butter and add the salt. Let stand until lukewarm.

Now blend the yeast sponge and the butter-and-milk mixture together in a large mixing bowl. Add the flour, cup by cup, and stir until you have dough. Put the dough into a large buttered bowl, cover with a towel and let rise for about 1 hour or until it has doubled in bulk.

Meanwhile, mince the onions and chop the walnuts.

After the dough has risen, add the onions and walnuts and blend well. Place the dough on a lightly floured work surface and knead, adding more flour if necessary. Divide the dough into 4 equal pieces, shape them into round loaves and place them, 2 each, on baking sheets that have been buttered.

Cover again with a towel and let rise for 45 to 60 minutes in a warm place.

Bake for 40 to 45 minutes or until nicely brown.

Cool on a rack.

ZWIEBEL KUCHEN
Onion Bread

Here is Germany's equivalent to Italy's pizza and France's quiche Lorraine. It looks a little like both and tastes delicious.

Serve this bread with fresh walnuts, and if you can get it, Black Forest ham and new white wine.

Yield: 1 large or 2 smaller breads. Can be frozen.

Dough:

1 envelope yeast	4 to 4½ cups flour
1½ cups milk	1 tsp. salt
½ tsp. sugar	

Topping:

½ stick butter	1 Tbs. salt
2 pounds onions	2 Tbs. caraway seeds
3 eggs	¾ cup finely-cubed smoked
4 Tbs. flour	ham (optional)
½ cup sour cream	

Preheat the oven to 375 degrees.

Proof the yeast in the milk that has been scalded and cooled to lukewarm, add the sugar and 1½ cups of the flour, cover with a towel and let stand for 1 hour.

Now beat in the salt and the rest of the flour. Transfer to your lightly floured work surface and knead until shiny.

Place the dough in a large buttered bowl, cover with a towel and let rise until doubled in bulk, about 1 hour.

Meanwhile, melt the butter in a fairly large saucepan. Chop the onions and cook them in the butter for 30 minutes, covered, over low heat. Do not let the onions brown. Take off the heat.

Beat the eggs until they are a light yellow; add the eggs, the flour, sour cream, salt and caraway seeds to the cooked onions and stir.

Butter an (18″ by 9″) baking pan or two (9″ by 9″) pans and roll out the dough to fit into the pan or pans. Shape the dough up a bit around the edges and let it rise for 15 to 20 minutes.

Now spoon the onion mixture and cubed ham over the dough, place in the oven and bake until golden, about 30 minutes.

Cool on a rack. Serve warm or cold.

KARIN'S WHOLE-WHEAT BREAD

This is just about the greatest dough to handle! It is so smooth and pliable and wonderful to knead that you will not want to let go of it, which is just as well; for the more you knead it the better the bread.

Yield: 2 large loaves. Can be frozen.

½ medium size potato
2 cups water
1 envelope yeast
½ tsp. sugar
⅓ cup light brown sugar
2 Tbs. salt

½ stick butter
3 Tbs. lard
⅓ cup molasses
4 cups whole-wheat flour
2 to 2½ cups all-purpose
    flour

Preheat the oven to 375 degrees.

Peel and cut the potato into small pieces. Put in a pot with the 2 cups of water. Bring to a boil and cook about 15 minutes until the potato is soft. Let cool to lukewarm, then put the potato and potato water in the blender and blend until liquified.

While the potato liquid is lukewarm add the yeast with the ½ teaspoon of sugar, cover and let stand until you have a yeast sponge.

Now add the light brown sugar and salt to the yeast sponge.

Melt the butter with the lard and stir the molasses into the melted fat. When this has cooled, stir the melted mixture into the yeast sponge, add the whole-wheat flour and about 2 cups of the all-purpose flour. Mix until you have a dough that holds together. When it is not sticky anymore, place the dough on a lightly floured work surface and knead it well, adding more of the all-purpose flour if it is sticky. Knead the dough until very shiny and smooth.

Put the dough in a large, buttered bowl, cover with a towel, and let stand in a warm place to rise until doubled in bulk, which will take about 1 hour.

Place the dough on the floured work surface, punch down a few times and knead again for a few minutes.

Divide the dough into 2 equal pieces and place in 2 large loaf pans (9" by 5"), cover and let stand to rise until doubled in size. This should take about 45 to 60 minutes.

Bake in the oven for 35 to 40 minutes or until the tops are browned and the breads sound hollow when tapped with your finger.

Brush the breads with water after you remove them from the oven.

These breads have a beautiful appetizing brown hue and a wonderful texture.

Cool wrapped in a towel.

BARBARI BREAD

The right bread to serve with a Middle Eastern meal. The sesame seeds (*barbari* in Iran) and the oil give the bread its delicate flavor.

Yield: 2 breads. Do not freeze.

1 envelope yeast	3 to 3½ cups flour
1 cup lukewarm water	2 Tbs. melted butter
2 Tbs. salad oil (not olive oil)	2 Tbs. sesame seeds

Preheat the oven to 375 degrees.

Dissolve the yeast in the warm water. Add the salad oil and stir. Add the flour a little at a time, stirring and mixing until you have a well-blended, manageable dough.

Place the dough in a large, oiled bowl, cover, and place in a warm area to rise for 1 hour.

Take the dough, knead it a couple of times and divide in two. Oil 2 baking sheets, and with your hands flatten and shape the 2 pieces of dough into 2 oblong loaves, ¼″ thick. With the edge of your hand make 3 ridges lengthwise on the surface of the dough.

Brush with the melted butter and sprinkle the sesame seeds on top.

Cover with a towel and let rise in a warm place for 30 minutes.

Bake for about 20 minutes until golden. Serve warm immediately. Or, later, reheat the breads by wrapping them in foil and placing in a hot oven for 5 to 10 minutes.

PANE ORIGANO
Oregano Bread

Although this is not the type of bread that you would serve at an elegant dinner, it is the perfect accompaniment for a picnic or a hearty meal outside in your garden. It is so attractive used as a centerpiece on a checkered tablecloth with a carafe of red Italian wine, salad, and perhaps a big platter of salami, mortadella and prosciutto.

Yield: 1 large loaf. Can be frozen.

1 envelope yeast
1¼ cups lukewarm milk
1 Tbs. salt
¼ cup olive oil

1 Tbs. oregano, dried
¼ cup freshly grated
   Parmesan cheese
3 to 3½ cups flour

For brushing the top of the bread:
2 Tbs. olive oil
1 Tbs. oregano, dried

2 Tbs. freshly-grated
   Parmesan cheese

Preheat the oven to 400 degrees.

Dissolve the yeast in the lukewarm milk. Add the salt and olive oil plus the oregano and grated Parmesan cheese. Stir in the flour, a little at a time.

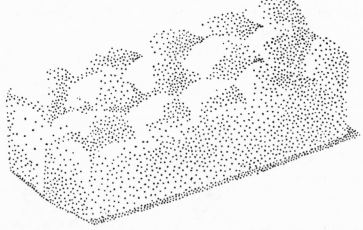

Turn the dough out onto a lightly floured work surface and knead until smooth and shiny.

Place the dough in a large oiled bowl. Cover with a towel and let stand in a warm place to rise for about 1 hour or until doubled in bulk.

Place the dough on your work surface and knead a couple of minutes.

Divide into 20 equal pieces and roll each into a ball. Butter a large (9" by 5") loaf pan, or better still, a loaf pan that is somewhat longer and narrower.

Place 14 of the balls in the bottom of the form in 2 rows, 7 in each row. Brush with the olive oil. Place the remaining 6 balls down the middle on top of the other 14. Brush with olive oil and sprinkle with oregano and Parmesan cheese.

Cover with a towel and let rise in a warm place for about 45 minutes or until doubled in size.

Bake in the oven for about 35 to 40 minutes or until the top is golden brown and the cheese starts to turn brown.

Serve warm.

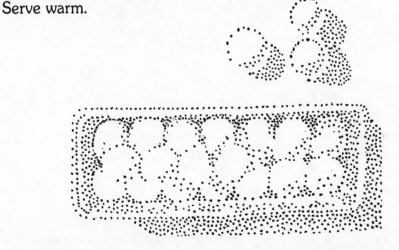

BREADS OF THE WORLD

PIZZA

Pizza, an ancient Roman snack, is actually bread with a relish. The relish can be just about anything, depending upon where you get your pizza.

Naples, however, is the great pizza city, where you find almost every combination.

Here is a recipe for dough which you can use with any of the fillings described. The dough is simple to make and provides enough for a 12″ pizza pan. Use unbleached flour.

Yield: 1 large 12″ pie. Do not freeze.

Dough:
    1 envelope yeast   1½ to 2 cups flour
    ½ cup lukewarm water   1 Tbs. olive oil to coat the
    1 tsp. salt   bowl

Preheat the oven to 450 degrees.

Dissolve the yeast in the lukewarm water. Add the salt and the flour. Knead on a floured work surface until you have an elastic, shiny dough.

Place the dough in a large bowl that has been coated with the olive oil. Cover with a towel and let rise for 2 to 3 hours.

Now turn the dough out onto a lightly floured work surface and punch it down a couple of times. Stretch and pull it into a round shape that fits the pizza pan, which has been greased with a little olive oil. Add the filling.

Bake in the hot oven for about 20 minutes or until done.

PIZZA NAPOLETANA

2 cups peeled, seedless tomatoes	4 anchovies
¼ to 1 pound mozzarella cheese (to taste)	1 Tbs. oregano
	¼ cup olive oil

Spread the chopped tomatoes on the dough, then add the mozzarella cheese and the anchovies. Sprinkle the oregano and olive oil on top and bake.

PIZZA CON FUNGHI
Pizza with Mushrooms

2 cups peeled, seedless tomatoes	½ cup freshly grated Parmesan cheese
2 cups sliced fresh mushrooms	¼ cup olive oil
	Salt and pepper

Spread the tomatoes on the dough, then the mushrooms and grated Parmesan cheese. Sprinkle the olive oil, salt and pepper on top and bake.

PIZZA CON CIPOLLE ED OLIVE
Pizza with Onions and Olives

¼ cup olive oil
3 onions
1 cup Italian pitted black
   olives
Salt and pepper

Brush the dough with some olive oil.

Slice the onions and cook them in the rest of the olive oil for about 10 to 15 minutes. Cover the dough with the cooked onions and the olives, and sprinkle with pepper and salt.

Serve immediately, piping hot.

CHALLAH

This recipe yields 1 huge, soft, wonderful challah. So moist that it will not dry out the next day, even sliced. Bake it fresh on Thursday and it will provide a beautiful touch to grace the Sabbath table Friday night.

Yield: 1 very large challah. Can be frozen.

2 envelopes yeast
1 cup lukewarm water
1 Tbs. sugar
8 to 9 cups flour
1 Tbs. salt
½ tsp. baking powder
1 tsp. cinnamon
1 Tbs. vanilla

½ cup sugar
3 eggs
¾ cup vegetable oil (not
   olive oil)
1½ cups lukewarm water
1 beaten egg to brush the
   top

Preheat the oven to 375 degrees.

Proof the yeast with the cup of lukewarm water and tablespoon of sugar. Add 6 cups of the flour and stir well.

Cover with a towel and let stand for about 45 minutes to rise or until doubled in bulk.

Sift together the rest of the flour, salt, baking powder and cinnamon, and add to the yeast sponge. Also stir in the vanilla, ½ cup sugar, 3 eggs, vegetable oil and the 1½ cups lukewarm water. Stir until well blended, then cover and let rise again for about 20 minutes.

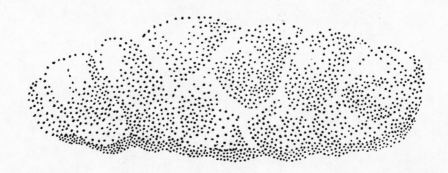

Now turn the dough out onto a lightly floured work surface, knead for a couple of minutes or until smooth and shiny.

Divide the dough into 7 equal pieces and roll each piece into a rope, about 12" long.

Place 4 of these ropes on a lightly oiled baking sheet and braid them together. Braid the 3 leftover ropes together on the work surface, then place them gently on top of the 4 braided ropes on the baking sheet. Cover with a towel and let the challah rise until doubled in size.

Brush with the beaten egg and bake until beautifully golden, about 45 to 50 minutes.

Cool on a rack.

WHOLE-WHEAT ANISE AND SESAME SEED BREAD

This loaf might taste good with couscous or some other North African lamb dish. It is also very good toasted with butter or made into a sandwich.

Yield: 2 small round loaves. Can be frozen.

1 envelope yeast
¼ cup lukewarm water
½ cup milk
1 cup water
1 Tbs. honey
1 cup whole-wheat flour
3 cups all-purpose flour

2 tsps. salt
2 Tbs. anise seeds, crushed
3 Tbs. sesame seeds
A couple of spoonfuls of
    cornmeal to sprinkle on
    the baking sheet

Preheat the oven to 400 degrees.

Dissolve the yeast in the ¼ cup of lukewarm water.

Scald the milk, add the 1 cup of water and the honey and let stand until lukewarm.

Meanwhile, in a large mixing bowl, sift together the 2 kinds of flour, add the salt, crushed anise seeds and sesame seeds.

Add the yeast mixture and the milk-water-honey mixture.

Mix well, then knead the dough on a lightly floured work surface until elastic and shiny. Add more all-purpose flour if the dough is sticky.

Place the dough in a large greased bowl, cover and let rise in a warm place for about 40 minutes or until doubled in bulk.

Take the dough out and knead for a couple of minutes. Divide into 2 equal pieces and shape each into a round bun. Place the 2 buns on a baking sheet that has been sprinkled with the cornmeal.

Cover with a towel and let rise until doubled in size, which should take about 1 hour.

Bake in the oven for about 20 minutes or until light brown and the loaves sound hollow when tapped with your finger.

Cool on a rack.

SFENJ
Doughnuts

Serve these doughnuts fresh and hot with heavily sweetened morning tea, like the Moroccans do.

Or sprinkle some confectioners' sugar on top and they will taste almost like our good old American doughnuts!

Yield: About 16 doughnuts. Do not freeze.

1 envelope yeast
1½ cups lukewarm water
1 tsp. vegetable oil
3 to 3½ cups flour

Dash of salt
About 2 cups vegetable oil
   for frying

Dissolve the yeast in the lukewarm water. Add the vegetable oil and flour and blend until you have a dough.

Turn out onto a lightly floured work surface and knead until smooth. Place the dough in a large oiled bowl, cover with a towel and let stand in a warm place to rise for about 1 hour or until doubled in bulk.

Take the dough out and knead for a few minutes. Cut off little pieces about the size of an egg, and roll them with your hands into little buns. Then poke a hole through each one with your finger.

Heat the oil in a deep skillet, but not too hot, since the doughnuts will get too brown on the outside while remaining unbaked on the inside.

Place about 3 or 4 doughnuts in the hot oil and fry on both sides until golden brown. Continue this process until all are done. Drain on paper towels and serve warm as suggested above.

LEFSE

This is the appropriate bread to serve at a smorgasbord. It is exceptionally good when buttered and accompanied by herring dishes or hard cheeses along with beer or aquavit.

Yield: 4 large flat breads. Can be frozen.

1 envelope yeast
½ cup lukewarm water
½ cup lard
1½ cups milk
⅓ cup dark corn syrup

1 Tbs. salt
1 Tbs. crushed anise seeds
1 Tbs. crushed fennel seeds
3 cups rye flour
2 cups all-purpose flour

Preheat the oven to 400 degrees.

Dissolve the yeast in the water.

Melt the lard over low heat in a saucepan. Add the milk and syrup and heat again until lukewarm. Add this to the yeast mixture along with the salt, anise and fennel. Stir in the rye flour and the all-purpose flour.

After the dough is well blended, turn it out onto a lightly floured work surface; knead until shiny and no longer sticky but still rather soft.

Place the dough in a large buttered bowl, cover with a towel and let rise in a warm place for about 1 hour or until doubled in bulk.

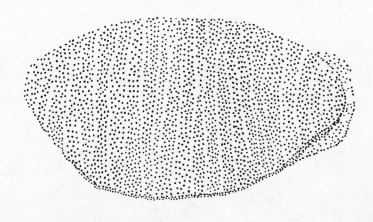

Again place the dough on the work surface, punch it down a couple of times and divide into 4 equal pieces.

Roll each piece out into a circle about 10" to 12" in diameter and, if you have a rolling pin with a waffle-like pattern, roll it over the flattened pieces so that you get a design; otherwise use the tines of a fork to make a pattern of little holes on the bread.

Place on buttered baking sheets, 1 bread to each baking sheet, and put in the oven at once.

Bake until light brown spots appear, which should take about 15 to 20 minutes.

Cool on a rack.

SABINA BREAD

Slice this bread thinly, add a good cut of ham spread with mustard, and you have a tasty sandwich indeed!

The syrup in this bread makes it a bit moist but still easy to slice.

Yield: 2 small loaves. Can be frozen.

1½ envelopes yeast
½ cup lukewarm water
1½ cups water
⅓ cup dark corn syrup
4 cups rye flour

2 cups all-purpose flour
2 tsps. salt
¼ cup warm water mixed
    with 1 Tbs. dark corn
    syrup for brushing

Preheat the oven to 400 degrees.

Dissolve the yeast in the lukewarm water.

Combine the 1½ cups of water with the corn syrup, and bring to a boil. Turn off the heat and let stand until lukewarm.

In a large bowl mix together the yeast mixture with the water and corn syrup. Add the rye flour, 1 cup of the all-purpose flour and the salt. Beat until shiny and then place the dough in a large buttered bowl, cover with a towel and let rise for about 1 hour or until doubled in bulk.

Now place the dough on a lightly floured work surface and knead in the rest of the all-purpose flour, kneading until elastic and shiny.

Divide the dough into 2 equal pieces, shape these into 2 loaves and place in 2 buttered loaf pans (8" by 4").

Cover with a towel and let rise for about 20 minutes.

Just before baking, brush the loaves with the water-and-corn syrup mixture.

Bake in the oven for about 30 minutes, or until the tops are golden brown and the loaves sound hollow when tapped with your finger.

Let the breads cool in the pans.

BROA
Corn Bread

This is a coarse bread, with a faint taste of olive oil. I would suggest serving it with a hearty Portuguese soup, such as *Caldo verde*, or kale soup as it is known in English.

Yield: 1 round loaf. Can be frozen.

1½ cups white cornmeal
2 tsps. salt
1 cup boiling water
2 Tbs. olive oil

1 envelope yeast
½ tsp. sugar
½ cup lukewarm water
1½ cups all-purpose flour

Preheat the oven to 375 degrees.

Before beginning this bread it is necessary to blend the cornmeal (preferably in an electric blender) until you have a very fine meal. Put the cornmeal into a bowl, add the salt and pour on the boiling water. Stir until smooth and then add the olive oil.

Dissolve the yeast in the lukewarm water with the sugar.

After the cornmeal mixture has cooled to lukewarm, add it to the yeast sponge and then add the flour, a little at a time, mixing until you have a fairly stiff dough.

Brush a large bowl with olive oil and place the dough in it; cover with a towel and put in a warm place to rise for 1 hour or until doubled in bulk.

Turn the dough out onto a lightly floured work surface and knead until smooth; add some more flour if it is sticky.

Brush a round 9" cake form with a little olive oil and shape the dough into it. Cover with a towel and let stand for about 1 hour or until doubled in size, then bake in the preheated oven. Try to serve the bread warm.

WHITE BREAD

These loaves look so beautiful, so smooth, so serene. But do not use bleached flour. It doesn't do justice to the bread.

Spread with butter or enjoy it plain with your meals.

Yield: 2 round loaves. Can be frozen.

1 envelope yeast
1 cup lukewarm water
2 Tbs. sugar
1 cup boiling water

¾ stick butter
3 tsps. salt
5 cups flour or a little more

Preheat the oven to 400 degrees.

Proof the yeast in the lukewarm water with the sugar.

Mix the butter into the cup of boiling water. Let it stand until lukewarm. Add the water-and-butter mixture and the salt to the yeast sponge. Beat in the flour a little at a time until you have a dough that you can knead.

Place it on a floured work surface and knead until shiny and smooth.

Transfer the dough to a large buttered bowl, cover with a towel and let stand in a warm place to rise for about 1 hour or until doubled in bulk.

Now punch it down a couple of times on your work surface. Divide into 2 equal pieces and place into 2 buttered round 8″ cake forms.

Cover and let rise again until doubled in bulk—this should take about 45 to 60 minutes.

Bake in the preheated oven for about 30 to 35 minutes or until nice and golden brown on top.

Let the breads cool for a couple of minutes in the forms, then remove the loaves and allow them to continue cooling on a rack.

ALMA'S BLACK BREAD

An authentic dark bread is not easy to come by (the commercial ones are usually darkened with artificial color). This recipe, given to me by a great-aunt from Russia, makes a loaf that is truly dark and rich.

Yield: 1 large round loaf. Can be frozen.

1 envelope yeast
¾ cup rich coffee, lukewarm
1 tsp. sugar
⅓ cup molasses
¼ cup cider vinegar
½ stick butter
1 square (1 oz.)
    unsweetened chocolate

3 cups rye flour
1 cup all-purpose flour
2 Tbs. salt
2 Tbs. caraway seeds
½ tsp. crushed fennel seeds

Preheat the oven to 375 degrees.

Proof the yeast in the lukewarm coffee with the sugar.
   In a saucepan, combine the molasses with the vinegar and bring to a boil. Turn off the heat and add the butter and chocolate, allowing them

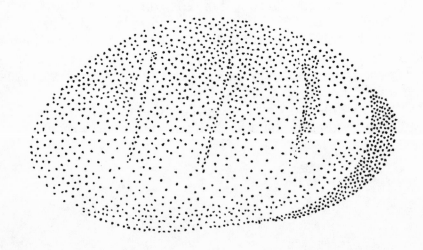

to melt. Let the mixture stand until lukewarm. Then stir in the yeast sponge and add the flours, salt, the caraway and fennel seeds. Stir until smooth, then place the dough on a lightly floured work surface and knead until smooth and shiny.

Place the dough in a large buttered bowl, cover with a towel and let stand in a warm place to rise for about 2 hours, or until doubled in bulk.

Knead the dough again for about 10 minutes, shape into a round loaf and place on a buttered baking sheet.

Cover with a towel and let rise for about 1 hour or until doubled in size.

Bake for about 25 minutes or until brown and the loaf sounds hollow when tapped with your finger.

Cool on a rack.

SCANDINAVIAN WHITE BREAD

This is an inexpensive recipe that yields 2 large loaves. Sliced thinly when it is at least a day old, it makes a very good base for a Scandinavian shrimp sandwich. Toasted and spread with butter and jam, it is great for breakfast. Try to get fresh (compressed) yeast for this bread; it does make a difference.

Yield: 2 large loaves. Can be frozen.

1 cake fresh yeast (2 oz.) or	2 Tbs. butter
2 envelopes dry yeast	6 cups flour
1 tsp. sugar	1 tsp. salt
½ cup lukewarm water	1 beaten egg to brush the
1½ cups milk	tops

Preheat the oven to 425 degrees.

Proof the yeast with the sugar in the lukewarm water.

Combine the milk and the butter in a saucepan and heat until the butter is melted. Let cool until lukewarm.

Into a large mixing bowl beat 4 to 5 cups of the flour together with the salt, yeast mixture and milk-and-butter mixture. On a lightly floured work surface knead all the ingredients until you have a rather stiff, shiny dough. You may have to add some more flour to the dough to get the right consistency.

Place the dough in a large, well-buttered bowl, cover with a towel and let rise until doubled in bulk, which should take about 1 hour.

After the dough has doubled in bulk, place it on a floured work surface and punch down a couple of times. Divide in half and knead each piece into an oblong loaf. Place both loaves side by side on a buttered baking sheet, cover, and let them rise in a warm place for about 25 minutes.

Before putting the loaves into the oven, brush them with a beaten egg.

Bake for about 30 minutes, or until they are golden and feel hollow when tapped with your finger.

Cool on a rack.

FULLKORNSBRÖD
Kasha Bread

A tightly-textured bread with a fine fragrance. Slice very thin and serve with butter and salami or cervelat as an hors d'oeuvre.

Yield: 2 small loaves. Can be frozen.

1 envelope yeast	1 Tbs. crushed fennel seeds
2 cups lukewarm water	1½ cups kasha
1 Tbs. salt	3½ cups whole-wheat flour
1 Tbs. crushed anise seeds	2 cups all-purpose flour

Preheat the oven to 375 degrees.

Dissolve the yeast in the lukewarm water. Add the salt, anise, fennel, and kasha. Stir in the whole-wheat flour and about 1½ cups of the all-purpose flour.

When the dough is stiff enough to knead, transfer it to a lightly floured work surface and knead until shiny and not sticky.

Place the dough in a large, buttered bowl, cover with a towel and let stand in a warm place for 1 hour or more until doubled in bulk.

Take the dough out, knead it for a couple of minutes and divide into 2 equal pieces.

Shape each piece into a loaf and place in 2 small buttered loaf pans (8″ by 4″). Cover with a towel and let rise in a warm place for about 1 hour or until doubled in bulk.

Bake in the oven for about 45 minutes or until the tops are slightly colored and the breads sound hollow when tapped with your finger.

Remove from the pans when completely cooled.

KRYDDLIMPA
Spicy Rye Bread

Kryddlimpa makes a flavorful sandwich base but is equally good just buttered. If you really like spices, double the amount in the recipe.

Yield: 2 large loaves. Can be frozen.

1 envelope yeast
2 cups leftover lukewarm coffee
½ stick butter
¼ cup molasses
2 pieces of pomerance (see page 19 for recipe)

1 Tbs. crushed anise seeds
1 Tbs. crushed fennel seeds
1 Tbs. salt
3 cups coarse rye flour (rye meal)
2 cups regular rye flour
1 cup all-purpose flour

Preheat the oven to 375 degrees.

Dissolve the yeast in the coffee. Melt the butter, stir in the molasses, and let stand until lukewarm.

Mince the pomerance (after you have softened it in a little boiling water), add to the butter and molasses, and combine with the coffee and yeast mixture.

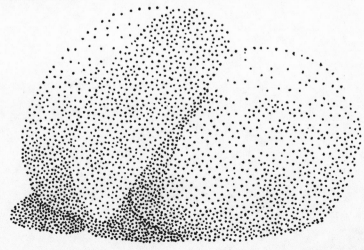

Add the anise seeds, fennel seeds and salt, and stir, while adding the coarse and regular rye flour and half the all-purpose flour.

Blend well, then turn the dough out onto a lightly floured work surface and knead until elastic and shiny, adding more all-purpose flour if the dough is too sticky.

Place the dough in a large buttered bowl, cover with a towel and let stand in a warm place to rise for about 1½ hours or until doubled in bulk.

Take the dough out onto your work surface and knead for about 5 minutes. Divide into 2 equal pieces. Roll and shape each piece into a round loaf; place them next to each other on a lightly buttered baking sheet. Cover with a towel and let stand in a warm place until doubled in size, about 45 to 60 minutes.

Bake about 45 minutes until brown and the breads sound hollow when tapped with your finger.

Cool wrapped in a towel.

RÅGKAKOR
Rye Bread

Use your leftover coffee, potato water or even hot chocolate or sour milk for this bread. It is wonderful fresh from the oven, spread with butter and served with a glass of ice-cold milk. It keeps well, too, and is a great base for a sandwich.

Yield: 2 round loaves and 2 tiny buns for the children. Can be frozen.

1 envelope yeast
¼ cup lukewarm water
1 cup liquid, as suggested
    above (Mix with water, if
    necessary, to get 1 cup
    of liquid)
½ stick butter or ¼ cup lard

¼ cup dark corn syrup
1 tsp. salt
2 Tbs. crushed fennel seeds
3 cups rye flour
1 to 1½ cups all-purpose
    flour

Preheat the oven to 425 degrees.

Dissolve the yeast in the lukewarm water.

Scald the 1 cup of flavored liquid. Add the butter or lard, salt, fennel and syrup, and let stand until lukewarm.

Pour the yeast mixture into a large mixing bowl and stir in the liquid-shortening-and-spice mixture. Then add the rye flour and half the all-purpose flour. Mix in more all-purpose flour until you have a dough that is not sticky.

Transfer the dough to a lightly floured work surface and knead for a few minutes until shiny and smooth.

Place the dough in a large buttered bowl, cover with a towel and let rise for about 1 hour or until doubled in bulk.

Return the dough to the work surface and knead for a couple of minutes. Divide into 2 equal pieces and shape these into round flat cakes, about 7" in diameter.

Place these on a buttered baking sheet and with a cookie cutter cut a hole, 1½" in diameter, in the center of each cake.

Cover with a towel and let rise for about 25 to 30 minutes. Before you place the breads in the oven, use a fork to prick random holes on top of the dough. Bake the cut-outs as well, as treats for the children.

Bake about 25 to 30 minutes until light brown.

After you remove the breads from the oven, brush them with water, then cool wrapped in a towel.

SUR-SÖTT BRÖD
Sweet-Sour Rye Bread

This bread with its rather strange sweet-sour taste is from the eastern part of Sweden. It is usually eaten with very spicy pickled herring and accompanied by a glass or two of aquavit. Butter and cheese also go well with it.

Yield: 2 large loaves. Can be frozen.

1 envelope yeast
2 cups lukewarm water
⅓ cup molasses
3 Tbs. vinegar

1 Tbs. salt
4 cups rye flour
2 cups all-purpose flour

Preheat the oven to 400 degrees.

Dissolve the yeast in the lukewarm water. Add the molasses, vinegar and salt, and stir.

Add the rye flour and some of the all-purpose flour and stir until you have a shiny dough that is not too stiff.

Transfer the dough to a large buttered bowl, cover with a towel and let rise until doubled in bulk.

Now turn the dough out onto a lightly floured work surface and knead until smooth and shiny, adding some more all-purpose flour if the dough is sticky.

Divide the dough into 2 equal pieces and place in 2 large loaf pans (9″ by 5″). Cover with a towel and let the loaves rise for 45 minutes.

Bake in the hot oven for about 30 minutes or until the tops are brown and the breads sound hollow when tapped with your finger.

When they are baked, remove the breads from the forms, wrap them in a towel and let cool.

BREADS OF THE WORLD

TUNNBRÖD
Thin Breads

This is the native bread of Lapland in the North of Sweden. It is somewhat reminiscent of the Jewish matzo, except it has leavening. The evening meal in Lapland often consists of these breads, home-churned butter, tiny fresh potatoes cooked in their jackets with dill, and some form of herring or dried reindeer meat—simple, but nourishing.

Yield: 16 very thin breads. Can be frozen.

1 envelope yeast
2 cups lukewarm milk
2 tsps. salt
2 cups barley flour

2 cups rye flour
Almost 1 cup all-purpose
  flour

Preheat the oven to 425 degrees.

Dissolve the yeast in the lukewarm milk. Add the salt and the barley and rye flour. Add the all-purpose flour, a little at a time, and mix until you have a firm dough.

Turn the dough out onto a lightly floured work surface and knead it for a couple of minutes. Without letting the dough rise, divide it into 16 equal pieces.

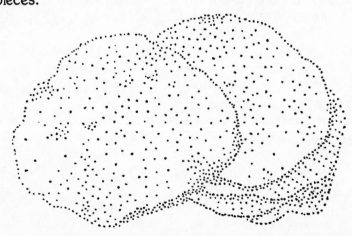

Roll each piece into a ball with your hands and place on a buttered baking sheet. Cover with a towel and let rise until the buns are doubled in bulk, about 45 minutes to 1 hour.

Now, with a rolling pin, roll each piece of dough out until almost paper-thin. Use plenty of all-purpose flour on your work surface so that the dough will not stick. The dough is easy to work with and will not break if you've mixed in enough flour.

If you happen to have a rolling pin with a waffle-like surface, roll over each flat cake to make a pattern. Otherwise, make a random pattern with the tines of a fork.

Place 1 or 2 thin breads on each baking sheet and bake at once in the oven for about 10 to 15 minutes or until the edges start turning light brown.

Cool on a rack. These breads taste good warm or cold.

PUMPKIN BREAD

A bread of unusual color and subtle flavor. Use fresh, cooked pumpkin; it is superior to the canned variety.

Yield: 2 small loaves. Can be frozen.

1 envelope yeast	2 Tbs. molasses
½ cup lukewarm water	1 cup mashed pumpkin
1 tsp. sugar	4 to 4½ cups flour
2 tsps. salt	¼ tsp. ground cloves

Preheat the oven to 400 degrees.

Proof the yeast in the lukewarm water with the sugar.

Add the salt and molasses to the yeast sponge, stir in the mashed pumpkin. Add the flour, cup by cup, and the ground cloves, stirring and mixing until you have a dough stiff enough to knead.

Place the dough on a lightly floured work surface and knead for about 10 minutes, until smooth and elastic.

Place the dough in a large buttered bowl, cover with a towel and let stand in a warm place to rise for about 45 minutes or until doubled in bulk.

Return the dough to the work surface and knead again for a few minutes. Divide into 2 equal pieces and place in 2 small loaf pans (8" by 4") that have been buttered.

Cover with a towel and allow to rise for about 45 minutes. Bake about 35 to 40 minutes until golden and the loaves sound hollow when tapped with your finger.

Cool wrapped in a towel.

DILL BREAD

Unusual flavor from the dill and onions—Moist texture from the cottage cheese—"Dillicious!"

Yield: 1 large loaf. Can be frozen.

1 envelope yeast
¼ cup lukewarm water
1 tsp. sugar
1 cup cottage cheese
1 egg
¼ cup coarsely grated onion
1 Tbs. melted butter

1 tsp. salt
¼ tsp. baking soda
2 Tbs. dill seeds
2 Tbs. finely minced fresh
  dill
2 to 2½ cups flour

Preheat the oven to 350 degrees.

Proof the yeast in the lukewarm water with the sugar.

In a saucepan, warm the cottage cheese until lukewarm, and add to the yeast sponge. Then add the egg, lightly beaten, the grated onion, melted butter, salt, baking soda, dill seeds and fresh dill. Stir until well blended, then add just enough flour to make a rather soft dough.

Put the dough into a large buttered bowl, cover with a towel and place in a warm spot to rise for about 1 hour or until doubled in bulk.

Remove the dough to a lightly floured work surface and knead for a couple of minutes. Then place in a large buttered (9" by 5") loaf pan.

Cover and let rise for about 30 minutes. Then bake in the oven for about 50 minutes or until the bread has turned light brown and sounds hollow when tapped.

Cool wrapped in a towel.

PLAIN ALL-PURPOSE YEAST DOUGH

An excellent dough that can be used for many different breads and rolls.

Yield: 2 large loaves or 20 rolls or buns. Can be frozen.

1 envelope yeast
¼ cup potato water (water in which you have boiled potatoes)
1 tsp. sugar

2 Tbs. shortening
2 cups milk (or water)
2 tsps. salt
About 5 cups flour

Preheat the oven to 400 degrees.

Proof the yeast in the potato water with the sugar.

Heat the shortening with the milk (or water) until lukewarm.

Blend the yeast sponge and the lukewarm liquid. Add the salt and the flour, cup by cup, mixing until you have a dough that you can knead on a work surface. Knead until shiny and elastic.

Place the dough in a large greased bowl, cover with a towel, and let rise in a warm place for about 1 hour or until doubled in bulk.

Take the dough out and knead it for about 5 minutes, then shape into loaves or rolls or buns. The loaves should be baked in two (9″ by 5″) buttered baking pans. For rolls, use muffin tins.

Bake 35 to 45 minutes until golden brown. Cool on a rack.

HERB BREAD

This is a firm bread that looks most attractive when thinly sliced. It is a nice accompaniment to cocktails and may be used as a canapé base.

Yield: 2 small loaves. Can be frozen.

Dough:
2 envelopes yeast
¾ cup lukewarm water
1 Tbs. sugar
1 cup milk

1 stick butter
3 tsps. salt
5 to 6 cups flour

Filling:
3 Tbs. butter
2 cups chopped scallions
2 cups chopped parsley
3 Tbs. fresh, chopped basil
2 cloves crushed garlic

2 eggs
1 tsp. salt
¼ tsp. freshly ground black
    pepper
1 tsp. Tabasco sauce

Preheat the oven to 375 degrees.

Proof the yeast in the lukewarm water with the sugar.
Scald the milk and add the butter and salt. Let cool to lukewarm.
Combine the yeast sponge and the milk-and-butter mixture in a large

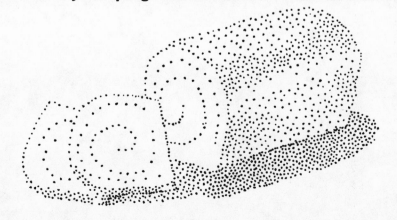

mixing bowl. Add the flour, a little at a time, until you get a rather stiff dough. Knead for a few minutes on a lightly floured work surface and place in a large buttered bowl, covered with a towel. Let rise for 45 minutes to an hour or until doubled in bulk.

Meanwhile make the filling:

Melt the butter in a saucepan. Add the scallions, parsley, and basil, stirring until slightly wilted. Add the crushed garlic and the 2 eggs, slightly beaten, stirring until the eggs begin to scramble. Season with the salt, pepper and Tabasco sauce.

Now turn the dough out onto your work surface and punch it down a couple of times. Divide into 2 equal pieces and roll each piece into a rectangle, about ¼" thick.

Spread the filling onto each rectangle and roll up like a jelly roll.

Place the rolls in 2 small (8" by 4") buttered baking pans, cover with a towel and let rise in a warm place for about 30 to 40 minutes or until doubled in size.

Bake about 45 minutes or until light brown and they sound hollow when tapped with your finger.

Remove at once from the pans and cool wrapped in a towel. Do not slice until completely cool.

RUTH'S PEANUT BUTTER BREAD

Even if your children do not like dark bread, the aroma of this wholesome bread containing peanut butter will change their minds. It slices well and is perfect for lunch boxes.

Yield: 2 small loaves. Can be frozen.

1 envelope yeast	¾ cup peanut butter
½ cup lukewarm water	1 tsp. salt
1 tsp. sugar	½ cup wheat germ
1½ cups water	½ cup evaporated milk
½ cup honey	3 cups whole-wheat flour
¼ cup molasses	About 1 cup all-purpose flour

Preheat the oven to 400 degrees.

Proof the yeast in the ½ cup of lukewarm water with the sugar.

Bring the 1½ cups water to a boil and, turning off the heat, stir in the honey, molasses and peanut butter. Then cook over medium heat until blended. Set aside to cool to lukewarm.

Blend the yeast sponge and the water-honey-molasses-and-peanut butter mixture together. Stir in the salt, wheat germ, and evaporated milk. Stir in the whole-wheat flour and about 1 cup of the all-purpose flour and then place the dough on a lightly floured work surface.

Knead until shiny, adding more all-purpose flour if the dough is sticky.

Place the dough in a large buttered bowl, cover with a towel, and let stand in a warm place to rise for 1½ to 2 hours, or until doubled in bulk.

Take the dough out and knead again for about 10 minutes. Divide into 2 equal pieces and shape into loaves.

Place these loaves in small (8″ by 4″) buttered loaf pans, cover with a towel, and let stand in a warm place to rise until doubled in size, which will take at least 1 hour.

Bake about 45 minutes until the loaves are brown and sound hollow when tapped with your finger.

Remove from the pans and let cool wrapped in a towel.

RUTH'S PEAR AND DATE BREAD

A very good bread created by a great cook who happens to be one of my favorite people. This is a flavorful and wholesome bread that is delicious for breakfast, spread with butter.

Yield: 2 large loaves. Can be frozen.

Dough:
1½ envelopes dry yeast	3 cups rye flour
2 Tbs. honey	2 cups whole-wheat flour
1 cup lukewarm milk	½ cup soy flour
4 Tbs. butter	1 tsp. salt
3 eggs, slightly beaten	

Fruit mixture:
4 to 5 pears, shredded (they should not be too ripe)	½ cup yogurt
	½ cup honey
½ cup chopped dates	½ cup chopped hazelnuts

Preheat the oven to 375 degrees.

Dissolve the yeast with the honey in the lukewarm milk. Melt the butter and, with the three eggs, add to the yeast mixture. Blend. Then add the rye flour, whole-wheat flour, soy flour and salt. Add the fruit mixture and blend.

Transfer the dough to a lightly floured work surface and knead until elastic and smooth. Place the dough in a large lightly buttered bowl, cover with a towel and let rise for about 1 hour or until doubled in bulk.

Knead the dough again. Divide the dough in half and place in 2 large (9" by 5") buttered loaf pans. Cover with a towel and let stand in a warm place for about 30 minutes. Bake in the preheated oven for about 35 to 40 minutes, or until the breads sound hollow when tapped with the finger.

Cool wrapped in a towel.

BREADS OF THE WORLD

SEVEN GRAIN BREAD

You can't really taste the seven different grains in this wholesome bread, but it's fun for the children to guess which they might be.

Yield: 2 large loaves. Can be frozen.

1 envelope yeast
2 cups lukewarm water
1 tsp. sugar
1 cup oats (not the quick-cooking kind)
2 eggs, slightly beaten
1 Tbs. salt
¼ cup honey

1 cup rye flour
1 cup whole-wheat flour
1 cup barley flour
1 cup all-purpose flour
½ cup rice flour
½ cup cornmeal
1 tsp. cinnamon
1 cup raisins

Preheat the oven to 375 degrees.

Proof the yeast in ½ cup of the lukewarm water with the sugar.

Pour the rest of the lukewarm water over the oats and let stand for about 10 minutes.

Mix the yeast sponge with the oat-and-water mixture, add the 2 eggs, salt and honey, and stir until well blended.

Add the rye flour, whole-wheat flour, barley flour, all-purpose flour, rice flour, cornmeal and cinnamon. Blend well and stir in the raisins.

Turn the dough out onto a lightly floured work surface and knead until shiny.

Place the dough in a large buttered bowl, cover with a towel and let stand until doubled in bulk, which will take about 1½ hours.

Knead the dough again on your work surface. Divide into 2 equal pieces, shape these into loaves, and place in 2 buttered loaf pans (9" by 5"). Cover again with a towel and let rise until doubled in size—about 1 hour.

Bake about 1 hour or until the tops are nicely brown and the loaves sound hollow when tapped with your finger.

Remove from the pans after 5 minutes, then cool wrapped in a towel.

6
SAVORY ROLLS & BUNS WITH YEAST

KAISERSEMMELN
Emperor Rolls

It's easy to get addicted to these with your breakfast coffee—they are that good! Break the fresh rolls, spread with butter and dribble a little honey on top. I guarantee that you won't be able to stop at just two, three, or four rolls.

Homemade, these taste as good as the ones you get in Vienna, but they may not look exactly alike because they are difficult to shape.

The malt extract, available in drugstores, health food stores, or specialty shops, gives the rolls their very special flavor.

Yield: 24 rolls. Can be frozen.

1 envelope yeast
1 cup lukewarm water
1 tsp. sugar
1 tsp. malt extract
2 cups flour
1 cup milk, scalded and
    cooled to lukewarm

1 Tbs. salt
3 cups flour
2 Tbs. cornmeal for the
    baking sheets

Preheat the oven to 450 degrees.

Dissolve the yeast in the water, add the sugar, malt extract and 2 cups of flour. Blend well. Cover with a towel and let stand in a warm place to rise for about 1 hour or until doubled in bulk.

Add the milk, salt and the rest of the flour to the yeast mixture.

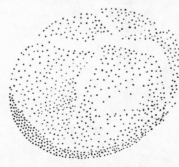

Place the dough on a lightly floured work surface and knead until shiny and smooth. Add some more flour if the dough seems sticky.

Place the dough in a large buttered bowl, cover with a towel and let stand in a warm place to rise for 1 hour or until doubled in bulk.

Turn the dough out onto the work surface and punch it down a few times. Break off little pieces, about the size of eggs, and shape into buns. Take each bun and pull 4 or 5 corners of the dough upwards, twisting to form a sort of topknot.

Place the buns on a baking sheet that has been buttered and sprinkled with cornmeal.

Cover with a towel and let stand in a warm place until the buns have doubled in size, which will take about 25 to 30 minutes.

Before you place the buns in the oven you can brush the tops with a beaten egg white, mixed with ¼ cup water, but this is optional.

Bake until light brown, remove from the baking sheets at once and cool on a rack.

PAEZINHOS DE CERVEJA
Beer Rolls

These exceptionally light and delicious rolls can be served as dinner rolls or with butter and jam for breakfast.

Yield: 18 rolls. Can be frozen.

1 envelope yeast
¼ cup lukewarm milk
3 tsps. sugar
½ cup beer at room temperature

About 3 cups flour
1 tsp. salt
2 eggs, separated
½ stick soft butter

Preheat the oven to 400 degrees.

Proof the yeast in the lukewarm milk with the sugar.

When you have a yeast sponge, add the beer, 1 cup of the flour and the salt. Mix until well blended; then place the dough in a large buttered bowl, cover with a towel and let rise for 1 hour.

Beat the egg whites until stiff and set aside in a draft-free place.

Then beat the egg yolks until thick and pale, beat in the soft butter, add the yeast dough and fold in the egg whites. Mix carefully until just blended, then place in a large buttered bowl, cover with a towel and let rise for 1 hour.

Meanwhile, butter muffin tins.

Turn the dough out onto a lightly floured work surface, knead it for a couple of minutes and divide into 18 equal parts. Shape these into balls and place in the muffin tins.

Cover with a towel and let rise in a warm place for 20 minutes.

Bake in the oven about 20 to 25 minutes until lightly golden. Serve hot or cold.

BREADS OF THE WORLD

KARLSBAD BUNS

At the turn of the century, these buns were served to visitors who came to the famous spa in Karlsbad, Czechoslovakia to take the waters for their health.

The buns are rather rich, with a bland taste that is a great accompaniment to a good English marmalade served with tea.

Yield: 24 buns. Can be frozen.

1 envelope yeast
¾ cup light cream, lukewarm
2 Tbs. sugar
¾ stick soft butter
2 egg yolks

½ tsp. salt
3 cups flour
1 beaten egg to brush the
   buns

Preheat the oven to 400 degrees.

Proof the yeast in the lukewarm cream with the sugar.

To the yeast sponge, add the soft butter, piece by piece, and the 2 egg yolks. Blend well. Add the salt with about 2½ cups of the flour. Knead on a lightly floured surface, working the dough until smooth but still rather soft.

Place the dough in a large buttered bowl, cover with a towel and let rise in a warm place for about 1 to 1½ hours.

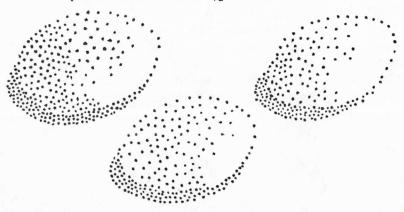

Dust your work surface with the remaining ½ cup of flour. Then turn out the dough and knead for a few minutes, working the flour into it.

Divide the dough into 4 equal pieces and roll each of these to a thickness of 1″. Cut each roll into 6 equal pieces and shape them into oblong buns with pointed ends.

Place these on buttered baking sheets, cover with a towel and let rise for 1 hour.

Brush the buns with the beaten egg and bake for about 20 minutes or until golden brown.

Cool on a rack.

CHEESE BAPS

Use either Cheddar cheese or Emmenthaler for these whole-wheat buns. Serve warm or cold as a sandwich base.

In England I have had these spread with cottage cheese, mixed with watercress, chopped cucumbers, parsley and a little pepper and salt.

Yield: 16 buns. Can be frozen.

1 envelope yeast
2 cups lukewarm water
2 Tbs. light brown sugar
4 cups whole-wheat flour

1 cup all-purpose flour
1 cup grated cheese,
   Cheddar or
   Emmenthaler

Preheat the oven to 400 degrees.

Proof the yeast in the lukewarm water with the sugar.

Add the whole-wheat flour and the all-purpose flour to the yeast sponge, and stir in the grated cheese. Blend well and knead for a few minutes on a lightly floured work surface. Place the dough in a large buttered bowl, cover with a towel and let stand in a warm place for about 1 hour or until doubled in bulk.

Return the dough to the work surface and knead for a couple of minutes. Divide into 16 equal pieces and roll each piece into a ball.

Place on a buttered baking sheet and cover with a towel. Let rise for about 30 to 40 minutes or until doubled in size.

Bake for about 20 to 25 minutes or until light brown.

Cool wrapped in a towel.

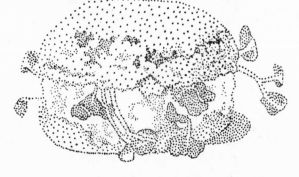

CROISSANTS

There are several different ways of making croissants, some more elaborate than others. This recipe is simple and makes good, buttery croissants that are crisp on the outside.

Naturally, you serve them with morning coffee!

Yield: 18 croissants. Can be frozen.

2 envelopes yeast	4 Tbs. sugar
¼ cup lukewarm water	1½ cups lukewarm milk
1 Tbs. sugar	2 sticks of butter
4 cups flour	1 egg yolk beaten with 1
1½ tsps. salt	Tbs. water for brushing

Preheat the oven to 400 degrees.

Proof the yeast in the lukewarm water with the 1 Tbs. of sugar. Add half a cup of the flour and mix together until you have a smooth ball.

Place in a buttered bowl, cover with a towel and let rise for about 1 hour or until doubled in bulk.

Meanwhile, in a large mixing bowl, blend together the remaining flour, salt, sugar and milk. Mix until you have a smooth dough, then

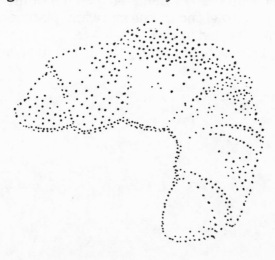

knead for a few minutes on a lightly floured work surface. Add the yeast mixture, blend and knead again until the 2 doughs are well blended. Place the dough in a large buttered bowl, cover with a towel and let rise for 2 hours.

Meanwhile, knead the butter with your hands until it is soft but still cool. Flatten it out into a rectangle; then put back in the refrigerator on a platter.

Now roll the dough out on the work surface to a rectangle about 18" by 12", pat the butter that you kept in the refrigerator onto ⅔ of the rectangle, but leave an area of about 2" of dough around the edges. Moisten the edges with some water. Fold the unbuttered third of dough up over half the buttered part. Fold the other buttered half down on top and pinch the edges together.

You have now folded the dough into thirds.

Give it a quarter turn to the right and carefully, with a rolling pin, roll out until you have an 18" by 12" rectangle. Again fold the dough into thirds. Wrap in wax paper or in a towel, place on a large platter and chill in the refrigerator for 2 hours.

Turn the dough again, roll out and fold as before into thirds. Repeat the procedure for a fourth and final time.

Put back in the refrigerator for another 2 hours.

Divide the dough by cutting into thirds, and leave 2 thirds in the refrigerator. Roll out the first piece into a circle about 12" to 14" in diameter. With a pastry wheel cut 6 wedges and roll each up, starting with the wide base side. Place on unbuttered baking sheets.

Do the same with each of the other 2 thirds of the dough.

Cover all with a towel and let rise in a warm place for about 30 to 35 minutes or until doubled in size.

Bake about 25 minutes or until golden. Try to serve these warm.

POGACSA
Biscuits

My whole family agrees that we are very fortunate to have neighbors such as the Razels. Lazlo Razel is Hungarian, loves to cook and bake, and sometimes brings us these biscuits to sample.

Yield: 18 biscuits. Can be frozen.

1 envelope yeast
¼ cup lukewarm milk
2 tsps. sugar
2 cups flour
1 tsp. salt
¾ stick soft butter
¼ cup sour cream

2 egg yolks, slightly beaten
1 cup crumbled crisp bacon
or finely chopped
crackling (optional)
1 egg, beaten with 1 Tbs.
water for brushing

Preheat the oven to 375 degrees.

Proof the yeast in the lukewarm milk with the sugar.

Add the flour, salt, soft butter, sour cream and egg yolks to the yeast sponge. Mix well. Then add the bacon or cracklings if you are using them.

Turn the dough onto a lightly floured work surface and knead until smooth. Shape into a ball and place in a large buttered bowl, cover with a towel, and let rise for about 30 minutes.

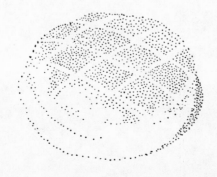

Return the dough to the work surface and knead again for a few minutes. Using a rolling pin, roll the dough out into a rectangle about ½" thick. Fold it into thirds and let rise in a warm place for about 30 minutes.

Roll the dough out again with a rolling pin until it is 1" thick, then cut out rounds with a biscuit cutter. Place the rounds on a buttered baking sheet. Use a knife to cut a lattice pattern on top of each biscuit, then brush with the egg and water mixture and bake about 25 to 30 minutes or until golden brown. Cool on a rack.

GRISSINI
Bread Sticks

Bunch these in a basket or a pottery jug; they look so decorative and taste like none you've ever bought in a store. Snack on them or nibble with a hearty soup or salad and, of course, some rustic red wine!

Yield: 22 bread sticks. Can be frozen.

½ envelope yeast
⅓ cup lukewarm water
⅓ cup lukewarm milk
1 tsp. sugar

2 cups flour
1 tsp. salt
4 Tbs. melted butter

Optional:
A soup plate with milk
¼ cup sesame seeds on a
   large platter

Preheat the oven to 450 degrees.

Proof the yeast in the water with the milk and the sugar.
When you have a yeast sponge, add one cup of the flour and stir well. Set aside in a warm place, cover with a towel and let rise until doubled in bulk.
In another bowl, blend the rest of the flour with the salt and the

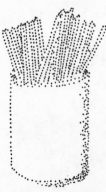

melted butter until you have a crumbly mixture.

Now blend the 2 mixtures together thoroughly until you have a smooth dough.

Place in a large buttered bowl, cover with a towel and let stand in a warm place to rise for about 45 minutes to 1 hour, or until doubled in bulk.

Take the dough out onto a lightly floured work surface, knead for a few minutes and divide into 22 equal pieces.

With your hands roll into thin ropes about 10" long, dip each rope into the milk and then roll in the sesame seeds. (If you omit this step you will have plain bread sticks.)

Place the ropes about 1" apart on buttered baking sheets and bake on the upper rack of the hot oven for about 12 minutes or until they are golden.

SMALL POPPY SEED BRAIDS

These look like tiny challah and children, especially, adore munching on them. The dough is the same as for the *zemmeln*.

Yield: 16 small braids. Can be frozen.

1 envelope yeast
¼ cup lukewarm potato
    water (water in which
    you have boiled
    potatoes)
1 tsp. sugar
2 Tbs. vegetable oil (not
    olive oil)

2 cups water
About 5 cups flour
1 beaten egg to brush with
¼ cup poppy seeds to
    sprinkle on top

Preheat the oven to 400 degrees.

Proof the yeast in the potato water with the sugar.
    Heat the vegetable oil together with the water to lukewarm.
    Blend the yeast sponge and lukewarm liquid. Add the salt and the flour, cup by cup, mixing until you have a dough that you can knead on a work surface. Knead until shiny and elastic.

Place the dough in a large oiled bowl, cover with a towel, and let rise in a warm place for about 1 hour or until doubled in bulk.

Turn the dough out and knead for about 5 minutes, then divide into pieces about the size of small apples. Divide each of the apple-size pieces into 3 and, with your hands, roll each mini-piece out into a rope, about 6" long and ½" thick. Braid the three mini-ropes together into a single braid. Continue until you have used all the dough.

Place on lightly oiled baking sheets, cover with a towel, and let rise for about 30 minutes.

Brush with the beaten egg and sprinkle with poppy seeds.

Bake about 20 to 25 minutes to a nice golden brown. Cool on a rack.

ZEMMELN
Rolls

Nice big crisp rolls that make excellent sandwiches.

Yield: 16 large rolls. Can be frozen.

1 envelope yeast
¼ cup lukewarm potato
    water (water in which
    you have boiled
    potatoes)
1 tsp. sugar
2 Tbs. vegetable oil (not
    olive oil)

2 cups water
2 tsps. salt
About 5 cups flour
1 beaten egg for brushing
Kosher salt, poppy seeds or
    sesame seeds to sprinkle
    on top

Preheat the oven to 400 degrees.

Proof the yeast in the potato water with the sugar.

Heat the vegetable oil together with the water to lukewarm.

Blend the yeast sponge and the lukewarm liquid. Add the salt and the flour, cup by cup, mixing until you have a dough that you can knead on a work surface. Knead until shiny and elastic.

Place the dough in a large oiled bowl, cover with a towel, and let rise in a warm place for about 1 hour or until doubled in bulk.

Take the dough out and knead for about 5 minutes, then divide into pieces the size of oranges.

Shape each piece of dough into a round 1"-thick roll. Make a rather deep crease in the center of each with a knife; place on a lightly oiled baking sheet, cover with a towel and let rise in a warm place for about 1 hour or until doubled in size.

Brush with the beaten egg and sprinkle with either kosher salt, poppy seeds or sesame seeds.

Bake until they are lightly browned and sound hollow when tapped with your finger, about 20 to 25 minutes.

ONION ZEMMELN

These are made exactly like the regular *zemmeln,* but you will need 1 cup of finely chopped onions. Sprinkle about 1 Tbs. of onion on top of each *zemmeln* before baking and proceed as above.

MARGARET'S SAMBOSAS
Meat-filled Buns

Nobody makes these spicy buns as well as my friend, Margaret Muiruri, the wife of a Kenyan diplomat and a great lady in her own right.

Whenever she invites me for afternoon tea—rich, dark Kenyan tea— out comes a large platter with these. They are out of this world, and disappear very quickly!

Yield: 20 buns. Can be frozen and reheated.

Dough:
- 1 envelope yeast
- ¼ cup lukewarm water
- 4 cups flour
- Pinch of salt
- 2 Tbs. corn oil
- 1 cup or more of water

Filling:
- ¾ cup ground round STEAK.
- 4 cloves garlic, crushed
- 1 tsp. ground cardamom
- 1 tsp. ground cloves
- 1 tsp. crushed cumin seeds
- 1 tsp. freshly grated nutmeg
- 1 tsp. cinnamon
- ½ tsp. white pepper
- ¼ tsp. black pepper
- ¼ cup minced Italian parsley
- 1½ cups chopped red onion
- ½ cup green peas
- ½ cup diced potatoes
- ½ cup minced green pepper, the small kind
- About 3 cups of corn oil for frying
- Lemon slices to serve on the side

Do not preheat the oven this time; the buns are cooked in oil in a deep fryer.

Dissolve the yeast in the lukewarm water.

In a large mixing bowl measure in the flour and salt and mix in the oil. Add the yeast mixture and a little water, mixing with your fingers until you have a soft dough. Place the dough on a lightly floured work surface and knead for 10 minutes. Return to the bowl and leave uncovered.

In a large bowl mix the ground meat together with the spices and the Italian parsley. Cover and let stand for ½ hour outside the refrigerator.

In a large frying pan, fry the onions in one tablespoon of oil until brown. Add the meat-and-spice mixture, green peas and potatoes and cook for about 15 minutes. Add the minced green peppers and cook some more, stirring until the liquids evaporate and the meat is fairly dry. Set aside.

Turn the dough out onto your work surface and divide into pieces the size of oranges. Place these on a lightly floured baking sheet, cover with a towel and let stand in a warm place for about 1 hour.

Now roll out each orange-sized piece with a rolling pin and with a knife cut into four wedges. Place about a spoonful of the meat mixture on each piece, fold the edges together and pinch so that they stay closed. Continue in this fashion until you have used all the dough.

Heat the oil to 375 degrees and deep fry the buns, about 4 or 5 at a time until golden. Drain on several layers of paper towel. Serve warm with slices of lemon.

FATAYIR
Spinach Buns

These spinach buns are always a success on picnics. They are not messy and can be eaten with the fingers.

It is also interesting to see how children like spinach if it comes in a little package!

Yield: 24 buns. Can be frozen.

Crust:

1 envelope yeast	1 tsp. salt
1½ cups lukewarm water	1 to 1½ cups whole-wheat
½ cup olive oil	flour

Filling:

1 small package frozen chopped spinach, defrosted and drained	½ cup pignolia nuts
	Juice of 1 lemon
	1 Tbs. dried marjoram
1 cup finely minced onions	⅓ cup olive oil
2 cloves of garlic, crushed	

Preheat the oven to 425 degrees.

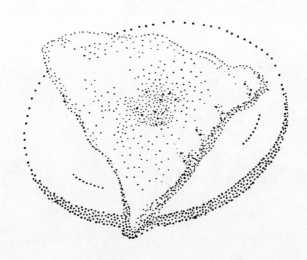

Dissolve the yeast in the water. Add the olive oil, salt and the whole-wheat flour and mix until you have a dough that you can knead. Knead for a couple of minutes on a lightly floured work surface, just until shiny and elastic.

Place the dough in a large oiled bowl, cover with a towel and let rise until doubled in bulk, about 1 hour.

Blend all the ingredients for the filling and set aside.

Turn the dough out on the work surface and knead for a couple of minutes. With a rolling pin roll it out very thin, but not so thin that it will break. Cut 4″ squares with a pastry wheel, place a heaping teaspoon of filling on each square and fold into a triangle. Pinch the edges together and place on a lightly oiled baking sheet.

Brush with a little olive oil and bake in the oven for about 20 to 30 minutes or until light brown.

Cool on a rack, or serve hot.

PANECILLOS
Rolls

Crusty rolls that are equally good for breakfast or dinner. Served with a spicy Mexican dish they are even more exciting.

Yield: 16 to 18 rolls. Can be frozen.

1 envelope yeast	2 tsps. salt
2½ cups boiling water, cooled to lukewarm	2 tsps. ground ginger
1 tsp. sugar	Cornmeal to sprinkle on the baking sheet
5 to 5½ cups flour	

Preheat the oven to 450 degrees.

Proof the yeast in the water with the sugar.

Stir 1 cup of the flour into the yeast sponge. Cover with a towel and let stand in a warm place to rise for 45 to 60 minutes or until doubled in bulk.

Blend together the rest of the flour with the salt and ginger and add to the yeast mixture.

Now place the dough on a lightly floured work surface and knead for a few minutes. Add more flour if necessary, and knead until you have a rather stiff, shiny dough.

Put the dough into a large buttered bowl, cover with a towel and let it rise until doubled in bulk.

Turn the dough out onto the work surface and knead for a couple of minutes. Roll the dough out into 2 long rolls; cut off pieces, the size of eggs, and roll each piece out into an oblong roll with pointed ends. Place these on a baking sheet that has been sprinkled with cornmeal, cover with a towel and let rise in a warm place until doubled in size.

Just before you put them in the oven, cut a few slits lengthwise into each roll with a sharp knife or razor blade.

Bake 15 to 20 minutes until they are a light golden brown.

Cool on a rack.

KHBOZ BISHEMAR
Filled Buns

Here is a slightly altered version of a Moroccan specialty that I first tasted many years ago on a visit to that country. They go perfectly with a glass of cold beer.

Yield: 5 filled buns. Can be frozen.

Dough:
1 envelope yeast	1 tsp. salt
⅔ cup lukewarm water	2 cups flour

Filling:
1 stick soft butter	¼ tsp. hot pepper, crushed
½ tsp. powdered cumin seeds	½ tsp. salt
1 Tbs. paprika (hot, if you have it)	¾ cup minced parsley
	1 cup minced onions
	1 garlic clove, crushed

Do not preheat the oven for these, since they cook on top of the stove.

Dissolve the yeast in the lukewarm water, add the salt and flour and mix. Knead until you have a stiff, smooth dough.

Place the dough in an oiled bowl, cover with a towel and let stand for 30 minutes.

Meanwhile make the filling.

Use a wooden spoon to work all the ingredients into the soft butter until well blended. Set aside.

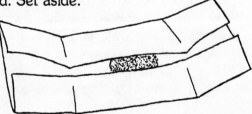

Turn the dough out and knead for a minute, then divide into 5 equal pieces. With a rolling pin, roll each piece into a very thin rectangle. Divide the filling and place 1 fifth in the middle of each rectangle. Fold the sides over lengthwise and with your hands flatten each filled bun out as flat as you can without breaking the dough; then fold the top down to the center and the bottom up to meet it and flatten out again.

To keep the finished buns from sticking to any surface while waiting to be cooked, place them on a floured baking sheet. Then heat a griddle or cast-iron frying pan over medium heat.

Place 2 or 3 of the pastries onto the griddle or pan and prick the tops with a fork so that some of the butter will seep through while cooking.

Cook each side until golden brown and serve warm.

KRINGLER
Pretzels

These soft pretzels can be served for breakfast. They smell and taste faintly of the cheese that's in them.

Yield: 30 pretzels. Can be frozen.

1 envelope yeast
2 cups lukewarm water
2 tsps. sugar
1 tsp. salt
1 Tbs. melted and cooled butter
1½ cups finely grated Swiss-type cheese (Norwegian Jarlsberg is great)

1 package farmer cheese, 7½ oz. or about 1 cup
5 cups flour
1 egg, slightly beaten, for brushing

Preheat the oven to 400 degrees.

Proof the yeast in the lukewarm water with the sugar.

Add the salt and the melted butter to the yeast sponge and stir in the 2 kinds of cheeses. Stir in the flour, cup by cup, and when well blended take out on a lightly floured work surface and knead until shiny and not sticky.

Place the dough in a large buttered bowl, cover with a towel and let rise in a warm place for about 1 hour or until doubled in bulk.

Take the dough out and knead again for a couple of minutes. Divide into 30 equal pieces.

Roll each piece into a rope about 12″ long and twist into a pretzel. Place on buttered baking sheets, cover with a towel and let rise in a warm place for about 25 minutes.

Brush with the beaten egg and bake in the oven until light brown, about 25 to 30 minutes.

Cool on a rack or serve warm.

BERGIS
Dinner Rolls

One does not always eat smorgasbord in Sweden. Sometimes there are sit-down dinners, and instead of Parker House rolls, these tasty little rolls might be served.

The dough is actually the same as for *frukostgifflar* but it is shaped and treated a little differently.

Yield: 32 small rolls. Can be frozen.

1 envelope yeast
½ stick butter
2 cups milk
2 Tbs. sugar
½ tsp. salt

4 to 5 cups flour
1 beaten egg
About ½ cup poppy seeds
    to sprinkle on top.

Preheat the oven to 400 degrees.

Place the yeast in a large mixing bowl.

Melt the butter in a saucepan, turn the heat off and add the milk and sugar to it. Heat until lukewarm and pour the mixture on the dry yeast.

Cover with a towel and let stand until bubbles appear on the surface of the yeast mixture.

Add the salt and the flour, cup by cup, mixing until you have a dough that you can take out and knead on a lightly floured work surface. Knead the dough until smooth, but still soft.

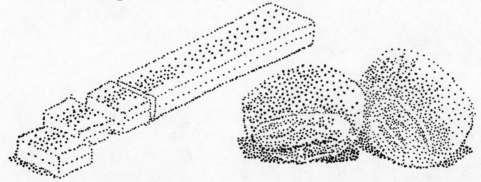

Place the dough in a large buttered bowl, cover with a towel and let stand in a warm place for about 1 hour.

Turn the dough out on the work surface and knead for a couple of minutes.

Divide the dough into 4 equal pieces. Roll each piece with your hands into a rope about 2" thick. With a rolling pin, roll each rope out flat until you have a piece that is ¼" thick and about 6" wide. Brush with the beaten egg and fold 1 third up lengthwise towards the middle. Brush the newly-exposed piece of dough with the beaten egg and fold the other side down so that you have a long flat piece of dough. Do the same with each piece.

With a knife cut into 1½" to 2" wide strips and place these on a lightly buttered baking sheet.

Cover with a towel and let rise in a warm place until doubled in size. Brush with some more of the beaten egg and sprinkle with poppy seeds.

Bake until golden brown.

Cool wrapped in a towel or serve warm.

FRUKOSTGIFFLAR
Breakfast Crescents

Serve hot for breakfast, with butter and jam.

Yield: 24 crescents. Can be frozen.

1 envelope yeast
½ stick butter
2 cups milk
2 Tbs. sugar
½ tsp. salt

4 to 5 cups flour
1 beaten egg to brush the
   tops
About ½ cup poppy seeds to
   sprinkle on top

Preheat the oven to 400 degrees.

Place the yeast in a large mixing bowl.

Melt the butter in a saucepan, turn the heat off and add the milk and sugar to it. Heat until lukewarm and pour the mixture on the dry yeast.

Cover with a towel and let stand until bubbles appear on the surface of the yeast mixture.

Add the salt and the flour, cup by cup, mixing until you have a dough that you can take out and knead on a lightly floured work surface. Knead the dough until smooth, but still soft.

Place the dough in a large buttered bowl, cover with a towel and let stand in a warm place for about 1 hour.

Turn the dough out on the work surface and knead for a couple of minutes. Divide into 4 equal pieces and make a ball of each piece.

With a rolling pin roll each ball out into a circle, about ¼″ thick and, with a pastry wheel or knife, cut the circle into 6 wedges of equal size.

Starting at the broad base of each wedge, roll up and then bend the tips until you have a crescent shape.

Place on a lightly buttered baking sheet and cover with a towel. Let stand in a warm place for about 35 to 40 minutes or until doubled in size. Brush with the beaten egg and sprinkle some poppy seeds on top.

Bake about 25 minutes until golden brown. Try to serve hot.

BREADS OF THE WORLD

CHICKEN BOREK

These chicken-filled buns make a very interesting and tasty accompaniment to drinks.

During the summer months when I have fresh mint and coriander, I add some, chopped, to the filling.

Yield: 12 filled buns. Can be frozen.

Dough:
1 envelope yeast	1 tsp. salt
⅔ cup lukewarm water	2 cups flour

Filling:
1 cup finely chopped cooked chicken	⅓ cup chopped walnuts
2 Tbs. finely minced parsley	1 egg, slightly beaten
2 Tbs. finely minced onion	2 Tbs. yogurt
¼ tsp. dried thyme	About 2 cups of shortening, such as the solid Crisco

Heat the shortening in a fryer until it is 375 degrees.

Dissolve the yeast in the lukewarm water, add the salt and flour and mix. Then knead on a lightly floured surface until you have a stiff, smooth dough.

Place the dough in an oiled bowl, cover with a towel and let stand for 30 minutes.

Meanwhile make the filling by mixing all the ingredients together with a wooden spoon. Set aside.

Take the dough and knead it for a couple of minutes and divide into 12 pieces of equal size. With a rolling pin roll each piece into a circle, about ¼" thick.

Place some of the chicken mixture onto the middle of each circle and fold over so that you have a crescent. Pinch the edges together.

Place on a floured baking sheet, cover with a towel and let stand for 15 minutes.

Now cook 3 to 4 buns at a time in the hot shortening until golden brown. Drain on several layers of paper towels and serve warm.

ENGLISH MUFFINS

Far better than any English muffins you can buy in the store, and much less expensive, too.

They are very easy to make and keep well. We like them toasted, buttered and spread with dark English marmalade.

Yield: 20 muffins. Can be frozen.

1 envelope yeast	1½ tsps. salt
½ cup lukewarm milk	1 egg
2 Tbs. sugar	4½ to 5 cups flour
1 cup milk	½ cup yellow cornmeal
½ stick butter	About 2 Tbs. butter, melted

Since you cook these on top of the stove, there is no need to preheat the oven.

Proof the yeast in the ½ cup of lukewarm milk with the sugar.

Scald the 1 cup of milk, melt the butter in it and let cool to lukewarm.

Add the salt and the slightly beaten egg to the milk-and-butter mixture.

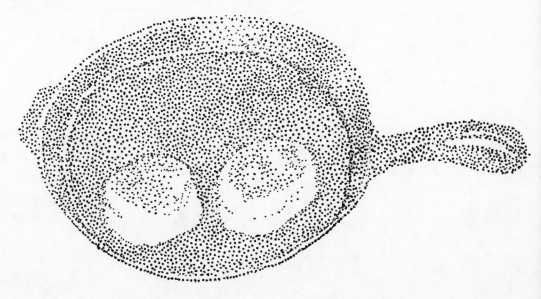

Pour the yeast sponge into a large mixing bowl and blend in the milk-butter-and-egg mixture. Add the flour, a little at a time, mixing together well.

Turn the dough out onto a lightly floured work surface and knead, adding more flour if necessary. Knead until elastic and shiny. Then place the dough in a large buttered bowl, cover with a towel and let rise for at least 1 hour, until doubled in bulk.

Meanwhile, pour the cornmeal onto a platter and set aside.

Take the dough out onto the work surface and knead again for a couple of minutes. Roll it out with a rolling pin to a thickness of about 1/3" and, with a glass or a large biscuit cutter, cut out round cakes. Put these onto the platter with the cornmeal, press down slightly and turn to get the other side covered with cornmeal.

Place on a baking sheet and cover with a towel. Let stand for about 20 to 30 minutes or until doubled in size.

Place a skillet over medium heat and when hot, brush with a little melted butter, turn the heat low and place about 5 to 6 muffins in the pan.

Cook for approximately 5 minutes on each side, or until they are slightly brown.

Cool on a rack.

Toast after they are completely cooled off and right before serving them.

GEORGIA RAISED BISCUITS

Two layers with butter in between make these delectable. The recipe is from a dear friend and a fine Southern cook, born and raised in Georgia.

Yield: 24 biscuits. Can be frozen.

1 envelope yeast
1½ cups lukewarm water
1 tsp. sugar
4 to 4½ cups flour
1 tsp. salt

1 stick soft butter
¼ cup melted butter
1 egg yolk and 1 Tbs. water
    for brushing

Preheat the oven to 425 degrees.

Proof the yeast in the water with the sugar.

Sift the flour with the salt and add the soft butter, piece by piece. Stir into the yeast sponge and mix well.

Take the dough out onto a lightly floured work surface and knead for about 10 minutes, adding some more flour if the dough is too sticky.

With a rolling pin roll the dough out to a thickness of ¼″ and with a biscuit cutter cut out rounds; place half of them on an ungreased cookie sheet.

Brush the tops with the melted butter and put the rest of the rounds on top of the ones with the melted butter.

Cover with a towel and let stand in a warm place to rise, until doubled in size, which will take about 40 to 45 minutes. Brush the tops with the well-beaten egg yolk mixed with the water and bake until golden, about 25 to 30 minutes.

Try to serve these warm.

CLOVERLEAF ROLLS

Same dough as for Parker House rolls, but with a different shape.
Lovely for dinner.

Yield: 20 dinner rolls. Can be frozen.

1 envelope yeast
¼ cup lukewarm water or
    potato water (water in
    which you have boiled
    potatoes)
1 tsp. sugar

2 Tbs. shortening
2 cups milk (or water)
2 tsps. salt
About 5 cups flour
½ cup melted butter
1 egg, beaten, for brushing

Preheat the oven to 400 degrees.

Proof the yeast in the water (or potato water) with the sugar.

Heat the shortening together with the milk (or water) to lukewarm.

Blend together the yeast sponge and the lukewarm liquid. Add the
salt and the flour, cup by cup, mixing until you have a dough that you
can knead on a work surface. Knead until shiny and elastic.

Place the dough in a large greased bowl, cover with a towel, and let
rise in a warm place for about 1 hour or until doubled in bulk.

Take the dough out and knead for about 5 minutes, then cut off small
pieces about the size of pecans. Make little balls, dip into the melted
butter and place 3 together in each muffin tin.

Cover with a towel and let rise in a warm place for about 30 to 45
minutes or until doubled in size. Brush with the beaten egg and bake
about 25 to 30 minutes until golden brown. Serve warm.

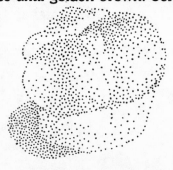

PARKER HOUSE ROLLS

Traditional American dinner rolls and we love them.

Yield: 20 dinner rolls. Can be frozen.

1 envelope yeast
¼ cup lukewarm water or
    potato water (water in
    which you have boiled
    potatoes)
1 tsp. sugar

2 Tbs. shortening
2 cups milk (or water)
2 tsps. salt
About 5 cups flour
½ cup melted butter
1 egg, beaten, for brushing

Preheat the oven to 400 degrees.

Proof the yeast in the water (or potato water) with the sugar.

Heat the shortening together with the milk (or water) to lukewarm.

Blend the yeast sponge and the lukewarm liquid. Add the salt and the flour, cup by cup, mixing until you have a dough that you can knead on a work surface. Knead until shiny and elastic.

Place the dough in a large greased bowl, cover with a towel, and let rise in a warm place for about 1 hour or until doubled in bulk.

Take the dough out and knead for about 5 minutes. Then with the help of a rolling pin, roll the dough out until it is ¾" to 1" thick.

With a 2½" biscuit cutter cut out rounds, make a crease in the center and brush with the melted butter. Fold in half and place in buttered muffin tins.

Cover with a towel and let rise in a warm place about 35 to 45 minutes until the rolls have doubled in size. Brush with the beaten egg and bake until they are an appetizing golden brown, about 25 to 30 minutes. Serve warm.

PRETZELS

You can make your own pretzels. They taste a little different from the ones you buy, but they are good, if not better.

Beer, of course, goes with these.

Yield: 24 pretzels. Can be frozen.

1 envelope yeast
1½ cups lukewarm water
1 Tbs. sugar
4 cups flour

1 egg, beaten, for brushing
Some kosher salt to sprinkle
    on top

Preheat the oven to 425 degrees.

Proof the yeast in the lukewarm water with the sugar.

Stir in the flour. Knead the dough on your work surface until shiny.

Place the dough in a large buttered bowl, cover with a towel and let stand in a warm place to rise for about 1 hour or until doubled in bulk.

Knead the dough again on a lightly floured work surface and divide into 24 pieces. Roll each piece into a rope, about 12" long, and twist into a pretzel.

Place on a buttered baking sheet, brush with the beaten egg and sprinkle with a little kosher salt. Bake at once until light brown, about 25 to 30 minutes. Cool on a rack.

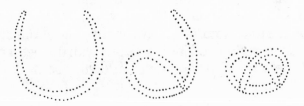

SOUTHERN POTATO ROLLS

Delicious "split-opens," very soft and buttery. Good either with breakfast or dinner or for tea with jam.

Yield: 24 to 30 large rolls. Can be frozen.

1 envelope yeast	1 tsp. salt
1½ cups milk, scalded and cooled to lukewarm	2 eggs, slightly beaten
¼ cup light brown sugar	1 egg yolk
2 cups cooked mashed potatoes	About 6 cups flour
1 stick melted butter	About ¼ cup melted butter for brushing

Preheat the oven to 450 degrees.

Proof the yeast in the lukewarm milk with the sugar.

Add the mashed potatoes to the yeast sponge. Then add the melted butter, salt, eggs, and yolk, and stir until well blended.

Add the flour, 1 cup at a time, until you have a dough that is soft but stiff enough to knead.

Take the dough out onto a lightly floured work surface and knead until smooth.

Place the dough in a large buttered bowl, cover with a towel and let stand to rise in a warm place until doubled in bulk. This should take about 1 hour.

Take the dough out and knead again for about 5 minutes on the work surface. Divide into 4 pieces and, with a rolling pin, roll each out to about ½" thick. With a biscuit cutter cut out rounds and place half of them in buttered muffin pans. Brush them with melted butter and place the other halves on top.

Cover with a towel and let stand in a warm place to rise until doubled in size, about 30 to 45 minutes. Brush the tops with a little melted butter and bake until light brown, about 20 minutes. Serve warm or cold.

7
SWEET BREADS WITH YEAST

FASCHINGSKRAPFEN
Lenten Doughnuts

These are like American jelly doughnuts, only better. They are light, yet filling, so after eating just 2 you'll feel very satisfied.

The important thing is to use good shortening for frying the doughnuts. I prefer the solid Crisco. Do not use oil. Also, try to get very thick apricot *lekvar* for the filling. *Lekvar* is Hungarian for a type of thick apricot butter which you should be able to obtain in a specialty shop.

Yield: 22 to 24 doughnuts. Can be frozen.

1 envelope yeast
½ cup lukewarm milk
1 tsp. sugar
1½ cups light cream
½ stick butter
3 egg yolks
⅓ cup sugar
½ tsp. salt

Grated rind of 1 lemon
About 5½ cups flour
About 1 cup apricot butter
   (or apricot jam)
About 3 cups shortening for
   frying
Confectioners' sugar to sift
   on top

Proof the yeast in the lukewarm milk with the teaspoon of sugar.

Scald the light cream, add the butter and let it melt. Then let it cool to lukewarm.

Blend the yeast sponge with the cream-and-butter and stir in the egg yolks, sugar, salt and lemon rind. Add the flour, a little at a time, stirring until well blended.

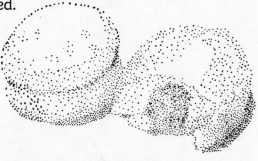

Turn the dough out onto a lightly floured work surface and knead until shiny and smooth. Add more flour if the dough is sticky. It should, however, be rather soft.

Place the dough in a large buttered bowl, cover with a towel and let rise in a warm place until doubled in bulk—about 1 hour.

Turn the dough out again and knead for a couple of minutes.

Divide into 3 or 4 smaller pieces for easier handling. With a rolling pin, roll out the dough until it is about 1/3" thick.

Cut out rounds with a 2½" biscuit cutter. On half the rounds, in the middle, place 1 teaspoon of the apricot butter. Place the other rounds on top and pinch the edges together well.

Place all the doughnuts on a lightly floured baking sheet, cover with a towel and let rise until doubled in size.

Meanwhile heat the shortening in a deep fryer to 375 degrees. Drop the doughnuts into the fat, 3 or 4 at a time, and cook for a couple of minutes, until light brown. Turn them over and cook the other side until light brown.

Remove with a slotted spoon and drain on several layers of paper toweling.

When cool sift confectioners' sugar over the doughnuts.

OMILLA'S BUCHTELN
Grandmother's Buns

One of my family's favorites. We like to eat these directly from the baking pan, breaking the buns apart while they are still warm, swimming in butter and absolutely divine!

Every second one is filled with apricot butter, all the rest with prune butter.

Try to get apricot butter (*lekvar*) and prune butter, otherwise jam will do.

Yield: 36 buns. Can be frozen.

2 envelopes yeast	2 eggs, slightly beaten
½ cup lukewarm milk	Grated rind of 1 lemon
1 Tbs. sugar	5 to 6 cups of flour
1½ cups milk	1 cup apricot butter (or jam)
2 sticks butter	1 cup prune butter
½ cup sugar	1 cup melted butter to pour
½ tsp. salt	over the buns

Preheat the oven to 375 degrees.

Proof the yeast with the lukewarm milk and tablespoon of sugar.

Scald the milk, then add the sticks of butter, the rest of the sugar and salt and let stand until the butter has melted in the milk. Cool to lukewarm. Add this to the yeast sponge, then add the 2 eggs, the grated lemon rind and the flour, a little at a time. Mix well, then place the dough on a lightly floured work surface and knead until shiny.

Add more flour if the dough is sticky.

Place the dough in a large buttered bowl, cover with a towel and let it rise for about 1 hour or until doubled in bulk.

Meanwhile melt the butter.

After the dough has doubled in bulk, turn it out on the work surface, punch it down a couple of times and knead for a few minutes.

Divide the dough into 3 or 4 parts, and with a rolling pin, roll each piece of dough out to a thickness of about ¼". With a pastry wheel or knife cut the dough into small 4" squares and spoon some apricot butter on every other square. Put a spoonful of prune butter on the remaining squares. Fold the dough over the filling, pinching the edges together so that the jam is completely enclosed, and place each little bun into buttered square baking pans.

Do leave some space between each bun, about ½", because they will rise and expand.

You will probably fill 4 (9" by 9") baking pans after you have finished rolling and shaping all the dough.

Now cover the buns with a towel and put in a warm place to rise for about 30 minutes.

Just before you put the buns in the oven pour the melted butter over them so that they are well covered. Bake until nicely brown on top; this should take about 25 to 30 minutes. Remove from the oven, but do not take the buns out of the baking pans.

Eat them directly from the pan while they are still warm.

You can also cover the cold buns with foil, pour a little melted butter on top and reheat them.

SOUR CREAM DOUGH

A very versatile dough that makes a fine, delicate and flavorful bread. My mother-in-law uses it for many different types of coffee cakes or just plain rolls.

For example, she puts the dough into a loaf pan and pokes about 2 cups of halved Italian plums or the same amount of pitted cherries into the dough.

This recipe makes 2 rolled up coffee cakes filled with apricot butter or *lekvar*; or you might want to use prune butter or perhaps a cinnamon-and-sugar mixture as a filling.

Yield: 2 small loaves or 20 rolls. Can be frozen.

1 envelope yeast
¼ cup lukewarm water
1½ sticks soft butter
3 egg yolks
¼ cup sugar
¼ tsp. salt
1 cup sour cream

About 3½ cups flour
1 cup apricot butter or
    lekvar or prune butter
    for filling
½ beaten egg to brush the
    tops

Preheat the oven to 375 degrees.

Dissolve the yeast in the lukewarm water.

In a large bowl, beat the butter, egg yolks, sugar and salt together, then add the sour cream and the yeast mixture and blend in the flour until you have a dough.

Now turn the dough out onto a lightly floured work surface and knead until shiny and smooth but still soft.

Place the dough in a large buttered bowl, cover with a towel and let rise until doubled in bulk. This should take about 1 hour.

After the dough has doubled in bulk, return it to the work surface and knead for a couple of minutes. Then divide into 2 pieces of equal size. With a rolling pin, roll each piece into a rectangle, about 8" wide by 14" long, and spread ½ cup apricot butter evenly onto each rectangle. Roll up in jelly-roll fashion and place in two small (8″ by 4″) buttered loaf pans.

Cover with a towel and let stand in a warm place to rise for about 30 minutes. Brush with the beaten egg before placing in the oven.

Bake in the oven until light brown, about 35 to 40 minutes. Let cool, wrapped in a towel.

This recipe will also be enough to make about 20 rolls.

STRIEZEL
Coffee Cake

If you prefer something that is not too sweet and cakelike with your afternoon coffee, then you must try this. Sift with powdered sugar if you wish, but it's not necessary. *Jause* is the word for afternoon coffee break in Vienna. Such a lovely custom!

Yield: 1 large coffee braid. Can be frozen.

1 envelope yeast	1 tsp. salt
⅔ cup lukewarm milk	1 tsp. vanilla
¼ cup sugar	1 cup raisins
2 eggs	1 cup slivered almonds
½ stick soft butter	½ beaten egg for brushing
3 to 4 cups flour	

Preheat the oven to 375 degrees.

Proof the yeast in the lukewarm milk with the sugar.

Add the 2 eggs, slightly beaten, to the yeast sponge. Also add the soft butter, about ¾ of the flour, salt, vanilla, raisins and almonds. Mix well until you have a dough, adding more flour as necessary.

Now turn the dough out onto a lightly floured work surface and knead until nice and shiny.

Place the dough in a large buttered bowl, cover with a towel and let stand in a warm place for at least 1 hour.

Return the dough to the floured work surface and knead again for a couple of minutes.

You are now going to make 3 braids, of graduating size.

Cut one-quarter of the dough off and set aside. Cut the remaining piece of dough into 1 larger and 1 smaller piece, so that you now have 3 pieces of different size.

Set the 2 smaller pieces aside and divide the largest piece of dough into 3 equal pieces, which you will roll out into three 12″ to 14″ long ropes. Braid these ropes together and place on a buttered baking sheet.

Take the second largest piece and divide into 3 equal pieces, roll into ropes, braid and place on top of the first braid. Finally, take the smallest piece of dough and divide into 3. Roll these into ropes, braid and place on top of the others.

You will now have a high, imposing braid. Cover with a towel and let rise in a warm place for about 40 minutes or until doubled in size.

Brush with the beaten egg and bake until golden and the braid sounds hollow when you tap it with your finger, about 35 to 40 minutes.

Cool wrapped in a towel. If you like, sift some confectioners' sugar on top when it is cooled.

TOPFEN KUCHEN
Cheese Coffee Cake

This recipe makes 2 cheese cakes. They are good, solid coffee cakes, and rather filling.

Yield: 2 cheese coffee cakes. Can be frozen.

Dough:

1 envelope yeast	2 cups milk
¼ cup lukewarm water	1 egg, slightly beaten
3 Tbs. sugar	2 tsps. salt
2 Tbs. butter	About 5½ cups flour

Filling:

1 pound farmer cheese	Grated rind of 1 lemon
2 egg yolks	2 egg whites, beaten until
2 Tbs. heavy cream	stiff but not dry
½ cup sugar	

Preheat the oven to 375 degrees.

Proof the yeast in the water with the sugar.

Melt the butter, add the milk, heat until lukewarm and add to the yeast sponge. Stir in the egg, salt and flour and blend until you have a rather soft dough.

Turn the dough out onto a lightly floured work surface and knead until elastic and not sticky. Place the dough in a large buttered bowl, cover with a towel and let rise for about 1 hour or until doubled in bulk.

Meanwhile make the filling: In a bowl, blend the cheese with the egg yolks and the heavy cream and sugar. Add the grated lemon rind, fold in the egg whites and set aside in a draft-free place.

Now return the dough to the work surface and divide it into 2 equal pieces; shape these into 2 oblong loaves and place in 2 buttered tube forms. Cover with a towel and let stand in a warm place for 45 minutes.

Now make a shallow ditch in both cakes and fill with the cheese mixture. Place the two pans in the oven and bake until the cheese starts to turn light brown. This should take about 30 minutes.

Cool on a rack.

VIENNESE KUGELHUPF

One of the great masterpieces of Viennese baking. Have a slice with your breakfast coffee. It is delicious!

Yield: 1 large round coffee cake. Can be frozen.

1 envelope yeast
¼ cup lukewarm milk
1 Tbs. sugar
1½ sticks soft butter
¾ cup confectioners' sugar
3 egg yolks
2⅔ cups flour

¼ tsp. salt
¾ cup milk
¾ cup light-colored raisins
½ cup blanched slivered
  almonds
Grated rind of 1 lemon

Preheat the oven to 375 degrees.

Proof the yeast in the lukewarm milk with the 1 Tbs. sugar.

In a large bowl, beat the butter with the confectioners' sugar until pale and fluffy. Add the 3 egg yolks, beating hard. Add the flour and salt, alternately with the milk. Add the yeast mixture and beat until well blended. Stir in the raisins, slivered almonds, and grated lemon rind.

Butter well a 6-cup *Kugelhupf* form or a 10″ tube pan and put the dough into it.

Cover and let rise in a warm place for about 1 hour.

Bake in the preheated oven for about 40 minutes or until it has a golden top.

Cool the *Kugelhupf* for about 10 minutes, then invert onto a platter and let it continue to cool, covered with a towel. When completely cool sprinkle with confectioners' sugar.

Kugelhupf tastes better when it is a couple of days old.

ZWETSCHKENKUCHEN
Plum Bread

Nothing compares to this on a summer's day, served warm, with a tall glass of ice-cold milk or iced coffee. Eaten outdoors, with the sun shining and the scent of roses in the air, it captures a bit of heaven on earth.

This is a recipe from my husband's Viennese grandmother.

Yield: 1 large bread. Can be frozen.

1 envelope yeast
½ cup lukewarm milk
½ cup sugar
1 stick butter, melted and
    cooled
2 eggs
½ tsp. salt

2½ to 3 cups flour
4 pounds dark blue plums,
    preferably the small
    Italian prune plums
½ to ¾ cup sugar to sprinkle
    on top

Preheat the oven to 400 degrees.

Proof the yeast in the lukewarm milk with the sugar.

Stir the melted butter, the salt and the 2 eggs, slightly beaten, into the yeast sponge. Add the flour, a little at a time, and blend until you have a dough that you can knead.

Turn the dough out on a lightly floured work surface and knead until shiny and not sticky but still rather soft.

Place the dough in a large buttered bowl, cover with a towel and let stand in a warm place to rise for about 1 hour.

Meanwhile, wash and pit the plums and cut into halves, as neatly as you can.

Return the dough to the work surface and knead for a couple of minutes. Then, with a rolling pin, roll the dough out into a rectangle that will fit a (17″ by 11″) baking pan that has been buttered. Place the dough in the pan and press the sides up a bit around the edges.

Place the halved plums neatly in rows all over the dough, leaving the edges free around the sides.

Cover with a towel and let stand in a warm place for 30 minutes.

Sprinkle with half the sugar and bake in the oven until the edges turn light brown, about 35 minutes.

Take out of the oven and sprinkle the rest of the sugar on top. Cool for about 15 minutes in the pan and then slice and serve. Can also be eaten cold.

VERVIERS BREAD

The secret of this famous bread lies in the lumps of sugar that you add to the dough, which give the bread its sweet, crunchy character.

Served warm with sweet butter, it will disappear in no time at all!

Yield: 2 small round loaves. Can be frozen.

1 envelope yeast	½ tsp. salt
¼ cup lukewarm water	2 eggs, slightly beaten
¼ cup sugar	4 to 4½ cups flour
1 cup milk	About 1 cup of small sugar
1 stick butter	cubes

Preheat the oven to 375 degrees.

Proof the yeast in the lukewarm water with the ¼ cup sugar.

Scald the milk, add the stick of butter to melt in the hot milk and add the salt. Let stand until lukewarm.

Blend the yeast sponge with the milk-butter-and-salt mixture, stir in the 2 eggs and add the flour, by half cups, stirring until you have a smooth dough.

Add the sugar cubes and turn onto a lightly floured work surface,

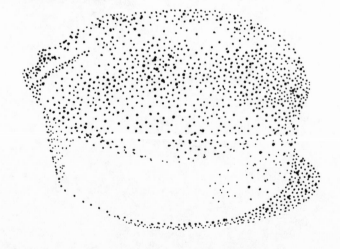

adding more flour if the dough seems sticky. Knead a couple of minutes to get the sugar cubes well incorporated.

Place the dough in a large buttered bowl, cover with a towel and let rise in a warm place until doubled in size, about 1 hour.

After the dough has doubled in bulk, knead for a few minutes on the floured work surface and divide into 2 equal pieces. Butter two round 8" cake forms and shape the dough into 2 round cakes to fit into the forms.

Cover with a towel and let rise again in a warm place for about 45 minutes.

Bake for about 30 minutes or until they are nicely browned on top. If you can, serve them warm!

FRUIT BREAD

Rich with fruit and Brazil nuts! If you serve this bread for Easter, bake it with a hard-boiled egg (in its shell) on top for decoration. Make a cross over the egg with some of the dough.

Yield: 2 large loaves. Can be frozen.

1 envelope yeast
¼ cup lukewarm milk
1 tsp. sugar
1¾ cups milk
1 stick butter
½ cup sugar
1 tsp. salt
1 tsp. cinnamon
3 eggs, slightly beaten
6 to 7 cups flour
Grated rind of 1 lemon

1 cup light-colored raisins
1 cup dried apricots, cut into small pieces
1 cup chopped Brazil nuts
¼ cup minced angelica (can be bought in a specialty shop)
1 Tbs. heavy cream for brushing
A little sugar to sprinkle on top

Preheat the oven to 400 degrees.

Proof the yeast in the lukewarm milk with the teaspoon of sugar.

Scald the rest of the milk, then add the stick of butter. Let melt and cool to lukewarm.

In a large mixing bowl, blend the yeast sponge with the milk-and-butter mixture. Add the sugar, salt and cinnamon. Stir in the eggs, 1 at a time. Add the flour, cup by cup, then add the lemon rind, raisins, cut-up apricots, chopped Brazil nuts and minced angelica.

Place the dough on a lightly floured work surface and knead until shiny and smooth. If it is sticky, add some more flour.

Place the dough in a large buttered bowl, cover with a towel and let rise in a warm place for 1 hour or until doubled in bulk.

Return the dough to your lightly floured work surface, knead for a couple of minutes and divide into 2 equal pieces. (If you are planning to make a cross, as in Easter bread, reserve a small piece of dough, about the size of an orange, for this purpose.)

Shape the 2 pieces of dough into loaves and place these in 2 large (9" by 5") buttered loaf pans.

Cover with a towel and let stand in a warm place to rise for about 40 minutes.

For Easter bread, place a hard-boiled egg, in its shell, in the middle of each loaf. Roll out the leftover dough into four ropes and make a cross over each egg.

Before you bake the loaves, brush the tops with cream and sprinkle some sugar.

Bake until nicely brown, about 30 to 35 minutes. Let cool in the pans.

Do not slice until the next day.

CANADIAN RAISIN BREAD

Spread with butter while still warm and enjoy this bread with tea.

Yield: 3 small loaves. Can be frozen.

2 envelopes yeast
½ cup lukewarm water
2 cups boiling water
3 Tbs. butter
1 cup light brown sugar
2 tsps. salt

1 cup molasses
2 tsps. cinnamon
1 tsp. nutmeg
½ tsp. allspice
About 10 cups flour
2 cups raisins

Preheat the oven to 400 degrees.

Dissolve the yeast in the ½ cup lukewarm water.

In the 2 cups of boiling water melt the butter, then add the brown sugar, salt and molasses. After this has cooled to lukewarm, mix with the yeast mixture, add the spices and the flour, cup by cup, stirring until you have a dough that can be kneaded. Add the raisins.

Place the dough in a large buttered bowl, cover with a towel and let rise in a warm place for about 1 hour.

Now turn the dough out onto a lightly floured work surface and knead for a few minutes until smooth.

Divide the dough into 3 equal parts; shape and place in 3 small (8" by 4") loaf pans. Cover with a towel and let stand in a warm place to rise for about 45 minutes or until doubled in size.

Bake in the oven for about 30 to 40 minutes or until they sound hollow when tapped with your finger.

Cool wrapped in a towel.

MÄHRISCHER KUCHEN
Moravian Coffee Cake

Luscious is the only word for this coffee cake. The filling will remind you of praline. You might try using pecans, almonds or filberts instead of walnuts in the filling.

Yield: 2 coffee cakes. Can be frozen.

Dough:

1 envelope yeast	2 cups milk
¼ cup lukewarm water	1 egg, slightly beaten
3 Tbs. sugar	2 tsps. salt
2 Tbs. butter	About 5½ cups flour

Filling:

1 cup tightly packed light brown sugar	½ cup finely chopped walnuts
½ stick soft butter	

Topping:

2 Tbs. heavy cream to brush the top	2 Tbs. chopped walnuts to sprinkle on top

Preheat the oven to 400 degrees.

Proof the yeast in the lukewarm water with the sugar.

Melt the butter, add the milk and heat until lukewarm. Add the entire mixture to the yeast sponge.

Stir in the egg, salt and flour and blend until you have a rather soft dough.

Turn the dough out onto a lightly floured work surface and knead until elastic and smooth but not sticky. Place in a large buttered bowl. Cover with a towel and let stand in a warm place for about 1 hour or until doubled in bulk.

Meanwhile make the filling by blending together the light brown sugar with the butter and chopped walnuts; set aside.

After the dough has doubled in bulk take it out and knead for a few minutes. Divide into 2 equal pieces and shape these into round buns which you place in 2 round 9″ buttered cake pans.

Cover with a towel and let rise for about 40 minutes.

Now, with your finger, poke random holes on top of the breads and place a little of the brown sugar filling into each cavity.

Brush with the heavy cream and sprinkle some chopped walnuts on top.

Cover with a towel and let stand for another 15 minutes. Then bake about 30 to 35 minutes until lightly browned. Cool on a rack.

CHELSEA BUNS

Wonderfully fruity buns that go well with tea.
Children love them; they seem to enjoy picking out the little currants.

Yield: 24 to 30 buns. Can be frozen.

1 envelope yeast	1 tsp. salt
¼ cup lukewarm milk	3 eggs
1 tsp. sugar	6 to 7 cups flour
1¾ cups milk	2 cups dried currants
1 stick butter	1 cup chopped candied
½ cup sugar	lemon peel

Preheat the oven to 400 degrees.

Proof the yeast in the lukewarm milk with the teaspoon of sugar.

Scald the rest of the milk, then add the stick of butter. Let it melt and cool to lukewarm.

In a large mixing bowl, blend the yeast sponge with the milk-and-butter mixture. Add the sugar and salt. Stir in the eggs, 1 at a time. Add the flour, cup by cup, alternating with the currants and lemon peel. Blend. Then place the dough on a lightly floured work surface.

Knead until shiny and elastic. If it sticks, knead in more flour.

Place the dough in a large buttered bowl, cover with a towel and let rise in a warm place for about 45 minutes to 1 hour or until the dough has doubled in bulk.

Turn the dough out onto your work surface, knead a couple of times and cut off pieces the size of an egg. Shape these into little buns.

Place on buttered baking sheets and cover with a towel.

Let rise until doubled in size, about 35 to 45 minutes. Then bake until light brown, about 20 to 25 minutes.

Cool wrapped in a towel.

BREADS OF THE WORLD

HOT CROSS BUNS

Hot Cross buns are usually served on Good Friday or, here in the United States, during the weeks preceding Easter.

They were originally pagan buns served by the Saxons as sacrificial offerings to their gods.

Yield: 24 buns. Can be frozen.

Dough:
1 envelope yeast	3 eggs
¼ cup lukewarm milk	6 to 7 cups flour
1 tsp. sugar	1 tsp. cinnamon
1¾ cups milk	1½ cups raisins
1 stick butter	1 egg yolk beaten with 1
½ cup sugar	Tbs. water for brushing
1 tsp. salt	

Glaze:
Confectioners' sugar mixed
with a little water

Preheat the oven to 400 degrees.

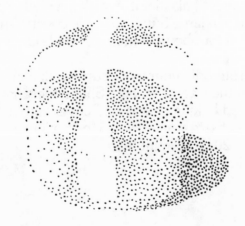

Proof the yeast in the lukewarm milk with the teaspoon of sugar.

Scald the rest of the milk, then add the stick of butter. Let it melt and cool to lukewarm.

In a large mixing bowl, blend the yeast sponge with the milk-and-butter mixture. Add the sugar and salt.

Stir in the eggs, 1 at a time. Add the flour, cup by cup, and also the cinnamon and raisins.

Place the dough on a lightly floured work surface and knead until shiny and elastic. If it is sticky, knead in a little more flour.

Place the dough in a large buttered bowl, cover with a towel and let rise in a warm place for about 45 minutes or until doubled in bulk.

Turn the dough out onto your work surface, knead a couple of times; then cut off pieces, the size of an egg.

Roll each small piece into a ball and place in a buttered baking pan, but not too close together, since the buns will rise and double in size.

Cover with a towel and let stand in a warm place to rise until doubled in size, about 35 to 45 minutes.

Before baking, brush the tops with the egg yolk-and-water mixture, place in the oven and bake until browned, about 20 to 25 minutes.

Cool on a rack. After the buns are completely cooled, dribble sugar glaze on the tops, making a cross design on each one.

POPE LADIES

These legless little ladies are traditionally served to welcome in the New Year.

Yield: 20 buns. Can be frozen.

1 envelope yeast	1 tsp. salt
¼ cup lukewarm milk	2 eggs
1 tsp. sugar	About 6 cups flour
1 stick butter	About ½ cup dried currants
¼ cup sugar	for decoration

Preheat the oven to 400 degrees.

Proof the yeast in the lukewarm milk with the teaspoon of sugar.

Scald the rest of the milk, then add the stick of butter. Let it melt and cool to lukewarm.

In a large mixing bowl, blend the yeast sponge with the milk-and-butter mixture. Add the sugar and salt. Stir in the eggs, 1 at a time. Blend in the flour, cup by cup. Knead the dough on a lightly floured work surface until shiny and smooth. Add some more flour if the dough sticks to your hands.

Place the dough in a large buttered bowl, cover with a towel and let rise in a warm place for about 1 hour or until doubled in bulk.

Turn the dough out onto your work surface and knead for a couple of minutes. Cut off pieces of the dough, the size of large oranges. Make torsos of half the pieces. Use remaining pieces to make a head and two arms for each torso. Do this directly on a buttered baking sheet.

Poke currants into each head for eyes and nose.

Cover with a towel and let rise in a warm place for about 20 minutes.

Bake about 20 to 25 minutes until light brown. Cool on a rack.

PULLA
Coffee Cake

The fragrance of this bread while baking is alone worth the work, but wait until you taste it! Perhaps served warm with some freshly brewed coffee.

Children adore it with a glass of cold milk.

It is easy to make and looks beautiful.

Yield: 2 braided loaves. Can be frozen.

1 envelope yeast	1 stick melted butter
1 cup scalded milk	1½ tsps. crushed cardamom
1 Tbs. sugar	4 to 4½ cups flour
2 eggs	1 cup raisins
1 tsp. salt	1 beaten egg for brushing
½ cup sugar	Sugar for sprinkling on top

Preheat the oven to 400 degrees.

Proof the yeast with the sugar in the milk that has been scalded and cooled to lukewarm.

After you have a yeast sponge, add the 2 eggs, slightly beaten. Then add the salt, the rest of the sugar, the melted and cooled butter and the cardamom.

Stir in the flour, cup by cup, until you have a rather loose dough. Stir in the raisins.

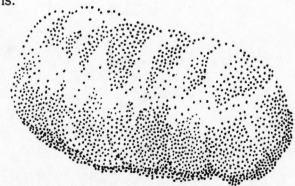

Place the dough on a lightly floured work surface and knead, adding a little more flour if it is sticky. Continue to knead until shiny and smooth. Divide into 2 equal pieces. Set one of the pieces aside.

Divide the other pieces into 3 equal parts and roll each into a rope, about 12″ to 14″ long. Place these ropes next to each other on a buttered baking sheet and braid them together.

Do the same with the remaining piece of dough.

You now have 2 baking sheets, each with a braided loaf on it. Cover these with a towel, place in a warm place to rise for at least 1 hour or until doubled in size.

Brush with the beaten egg and sprinkle some sugar on top.

Bake in the oven until beautifully golden brown, about 30 minutes.

BABA AU RHUM or ROMOVAYA BABA

It is not quite clear whether this culinary masterpiece originated in France or Russia, so I have credited both countries with this marvelous yeast dessert. I like to serve it with fresh strawberries or raspberries and whipped cream.

Yield: 2 cakes. Do not freeze.

Dough:

1 envelope yeast	1 cup sugar
1 cup lukewarm milk	½ tsp. salt
1 tsp. sugar	1 tsp. vanilla
4 to 4½ cups flour	1½ sticks soft butter
6 eggs	1 cup warm milk

Rum syrup:
    1 cup water
    1 cup sugar
    ⅓ cup dark rum

Preheat the oven to 375 degrees.

Proof the yeast in 1 cup of lukewarm milk and the teaspoon of sugar.

After you have a good yeast sponge, beat in half the flour until smooth. Place in a large buttered bowl, cover with a towel and let rise about 1 hour until doubled in bulk.

Meanwhile, divide the eggs and beat the whites until they are rather stiff. Set aside in a draft-free place.

Beat the yolks with the 1 cup sugar, salt and vanilla until pale and also set aside.

Now beat the butter until well creamed, add the yeast mixture and stir well. Then stir in the egg-yolk mixture, the other cup of lukewarm milk, and the rest of the flour. Fold in the egg whites.

You will now have a very soft dough. Place in a large buttered bowl, cover with a towel and let rise until doubled in bulk, about 45 minutes to 1 hour.

Meanwhile, butter 2 baba molds or other fancy, tall molds. Carefully pour in the dough and place in the oven.

Bake for about 1 hour or until a cake tester comes out clean.

While the baba is baking, make the rum syrup:

Heat the water with the sugar, stirring to dissolve the sugar. Turn off the heat and add the rum.

After you remove the babas from the oven, unmold them onto 2 soup plates and baste with the rum syrup. Continue to baste until all the rum syrup is used and the babas are soaked.

Serve with berries and cream.

You can also make 1 large baba in 1 big mold, but I get better results by dividing in 2.

CHOCOLATE BUNS

These are the chocolate buns that French children adore. Similar buns are found all over Europe, though each country makes a slightly different version.

In Austria the rolls are filled with grated chocolate, ground walnuts and raisins.

Yield: 30 buns. Do not freeze.

Dough:
1 envelope yeast
¼ cup lukewarm water
1 tsp. sugar
1¾ cups milk
1 stick butter

¼ cup sugar
1 tsp. salt
3 eggs
1 Tbs. vanilla
6 to 7 cups flour

Filling:
2 3½ oz. bars fine imported
    chocolate, bittersweet or
    milk, whichever you
    prefer

Preheat the oven to 400 degrees.

Proof the yeast in the lukewarm water with the teaspoon of sugar.

Scald the milk, then add the stick of butter. Let it melt and cool to lukewarm.

In a large mixing bowl, blend the yeast sponge with the milk-and-butter mixture. Add the sugar and salt. Stir in the eggs, 1 at a time, and add the vanilla. Blend in the flour, cup by cup. Place the dough on a lightly floured work surface and knead until shiny and elastic. If it sticks, knead in more flour.

Place the dough in a large buttered bowl, cover with a towel and let rise in a warm place for about 45 minutes to 1 hour or until doubled in bulk.

Take the dough out onto your work surface, knead a couple of times and cut into 3 pieces because it is easier to work with smaller pieces of dough.

Roll each piece of dough to a thickness of about ¼" and, with a pastry wheel or knife, cut 30 squares that are about 3" on each side.

Divide the chocolate bars so that you have 30 pieces and place 1 piece on each little square. Fold the dough over the piece of chocolate to cover completely and tuck the ends in underneath the bun.

Place on buttered baking sheets. Cover with a towel and let stand in a warm place to rise until doubled in size. This should take about 35 to 40 minutes.

Bake in the oven until light brown, about 25 to 30 minutes. Cool wrapped in a towel.

BERLINER
Berlin Doughnuts

But for the name and the raspberry jam filling, these are exactly the same as the Austrian *Faschingskrapfen* (page 141).

It is amusing to watch an Austrian and a German enter a *Konditorei:* one asks for *"Berliner"* and the other for *"Faschingskrapfen,"* but they both get the same dessert!

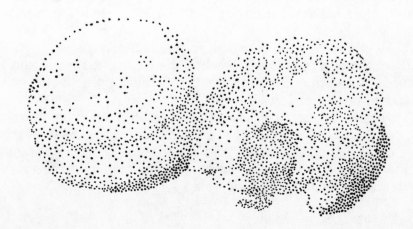

OLIEBOLLEN
Dutch Doughnuts

The Dutch like to serve these for New Year's. They are excellent with coffee and children enjoy them with milk.

Yield: 24 doughnuts.
Can be frozen but this is not recommended.

1 envelope yeast
½ cup lukewarm milk
1 tsp. sugar
1½ cups light cream
½ stick butter
3 egg yolks
⅓ cup sugar
½ tsp. salt
Grated rind of 1 lemon
About 5½ cups flour

2 cups coarsely grated
  apples
1 cup raisins
½ cup diced candied orange
  peel
About 3 cups shortening for
  frying (I prefer Crisco)
Confectioners' sugar to sift
  over the tops

Proof the yeast in the lukewarm milk with the teaspoon of sugar.

Scald the light cream, add the butter and let it melt. Then cool to lukewarm.

Blend the yeast sponge with the cream-and-butter and stir in the egg yolks, sugar, salt and lemon rind. Add the flour, a little at a time, stirring until well blended.

Now stir in the grated apples, raisins and orange peel.

Turn the dough out onto a lightly floured work surface and knead until shiny and smooth. Add more flour if the dough is sticky; however, it should be rather soft.

Now place the dough in a large buttered bowl, cover with a towel and let rise in a warm place until doubled in bulk—about 50 to 60 minutes.

Take the dough out again and knead for a couple of minutes.

Put the dough back in the bowl to rest while you heat the shortening. It should be heated to 375 degrees.

With a tablespoon drop pieces of dough into the fat (about 5 or 6 at a time) and cook until light brown.

Drain on several layers of paper toweling and sift confectioners' sugar over the doughnuts. Serve warm.

RUSKS

If you don't feel well or can't go to sleep, eat these with some warm milk. Dip them in if nobody's looking. So good and so soothing.

Yield: 60 rusks. Do not freeze.

1 envelope yeast
2 cups milk, scalded and
   cooled to lukewarm
½ cup sugar
1 stick and 2 Tbs. soft
   butter

About 6 to 8 cups flour
1 tsp. crushed cardamom
   seeds (optional)

Preheat the oven to 400 degrees.

Proof the yeast in ½ cup of the lukewarm milk with 1 teaspoon of the sugar.

When you have a yeast sponge, add the rest of the milk, sugar, and soft butter. Stir in the flour, cup by cup, until you have a dough that you can knead. Work until smooth and shiny, then place in a large buttered bowl, cover with a towel and put in a warm place for about 1 hour or until doubled in bulk.

Take the dough out onto a lightly floured work surface, knead for a few minutes and roll into ropes, about 2" thick. Break off pieces, about the size of an egg, and shape into little round buns.

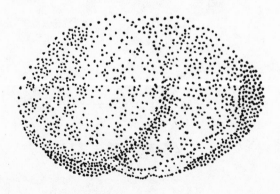

Place these on buttered baking sheets, cover with a towel and let rise until doubled in bulk, about 45 minutes.

Bake in the oven until they are pale gold, about 15 to 20 minutes. Cool on a rack.

After they have cooled, use a big fork to slice the top half off each bun. Place both tops and bottoms on a baking sheet; they can be rather close together.

Bake in a 400-degree oven until light brown, about 10 to 15 minutes. Turn off the heat and let them get crisp.

Let cool completely before eating.

These will keep crisp and fresh for a long time. If they do get soggy, put them back in a low oven and let them crisp again.

BARM BRACK

A fragrant tea bread that is particularly delicious when served warm and spread with butter.

Yield: 1 bread. Can be frozen.

1 envelope yeast	1 cup lukewarm milk
¼ cup lukewarm milk	3 Tbs. soft butter
2 Tbs. sugar	2 eggs
3½ cups flour	1 cup white raisins
½ tsp. salt	½ cup dried currants
½ tsp. nutmeg	½ cup chopped candied
½ tsp. cinnamon	lemon peel

Preheat the oven to 400 degrees.

Proof the yeast in the ¼ cup milk with the sugar.

In a large bowl, blend the flour, salt, nutmeg and cinnamon. Add the yeast mixture, the 1 cup milk, softened butter and eggs. Beat until smooth. Now add the raisins, currants and candied peel, and blend well into the dough.

Place the dough in a buttered 10″ tube pan and cover, letting it rise in a warm place for at least 1 hour.

Bake the bread for about 1 hour, or until it has a light brown color and sounds hollow when tapped. If the bread seems to brown too quickly, cover the top with a piece of foil.

After removing from the oven, let the bread stand in the form for 10 minutes before removing. Then cool on a rack.

MARITOZZI ROMANI
Roman Breakfast Buns

These buns are good with coffee in the morning, very good indeed.

This is a family recipe given to me by a relative from Italy. She has always made them this way, and though a simpler version might taste the same, I dare not try to vary it.

Yield: 24 buns. Can be frozen.

1 envelope yeast	3 Tbs. olive oil
½ cup lukewarm water	½ cup lukewarm water
4 to 4½ cups flour	⅓ cup sugar
½ tsp. salt	1 cup raisins
2 eggs	1 egg, beaten, for brushing

Preheat the oven to 400 degrees.

Beat together the yeast with the ½ cup lukewarm water and 1 to 1½ cups of the flour until you have a smooth paste. Cover with a towel and let stand in a warm place for about 1 hour, until doubled in bulk.

Measure 3 cups of flour into a large bowl, make a well in the center and put in the salt, the eggs, the olive oil, and water. Mix until well blended. Then turn out on a lightly floured work surface and knead until you have a shiny dough.

Now add the yeast mixture, kneading together until well combined.

Make a hollow in the center of the dough and add the sugar and the raisins, kneading again until smooth, shiny and evenly blended.

Place the dough in a large buttered bowl, cover with a towel and let stand in a warm place for about 1 hour or until doubled in bulk.

Take the dough out onto your work surface, punch it down a couple of times and roll into lengths. Cut off pieces the size of an egg and form these into round buns. Place onto oiled baking sheets, cover with a towel and let rise until doubled in size. This should take about 20 to 30 minutes.

Brush with the beaten egg and bake until golden brown, about 25 to 30 minutes. Cool wrapped in a towel.

PANETTONE

A light superb yeast cake that comes from Milano, where one can actually buy it from street vendors.

Here we can buy panettone in fancy shops, especially around Christmas and Easter, but once you have baked your own, you will know which is best.

Different cities in Italy have different versions of panettone; some use pignolia nuts, pistachio nuts or fennel seeds; some use no fruit or raisins at all.

My favorite is the real Milanese version, and here it is:

Yield: 2 breads. Can be frozen.

1 envelope yeast
½ cup lukewarm water
1 tsp. sugar
1 cup flour
2 sticks butter, melted and
    cooled
¾ cup sugar
½ tsp. salt
2 eggs
6 egg yolks

4 cups flour
1 cup light-colored raisins
½ cup diced candied lemon
    peel
½ cup diced candied orange
    peel
Grated rind of 1 lemon
Confectioners' sugar to
    sprinkle on top

Preheat the oven to 375 degrees.

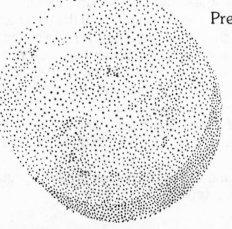

Proof the yeast in the lukewarm water with the spoonful of sugar. Stir in the cup of flour. Cover with a towel and let rise in a warm place for about 1 hour or until doubled in bulk.

Add the melted and cooled butter, sugar, salt, the 2 eggs and 6 egg yolks. Stir in the flour, the raisins, the diced lemon and orange peel and grated lemon rind.

Mix well and place on a lightly floured work surface. Knead until shiny and smooth.

Place the dough in a large buttered bowl, cover with a towel and let stand in a warm place to rise for 1½ to 2 hours.

Knead the dough again on the work surface and divide into 2 equal pieces. Form these into 2 balls, place on a buttered baking sheet, cover with a towel and let stand in a warm place for 2 hours.

With a razor blade cut a cross on top of each bread. Place in the oven and bake for 1 hour or until the breads are light brown and your cake tester comes out clean.

Cool wrapped in a towel and dust with confectioners' sugar after the breads are cooled.

PANGIALLO
Roman Christmas Bread*

Lots of nuts, candied fruit and spices make this compact, heavy bread absolutely "taste" of Christmas. It is to the Romans what panettone is to the Milanese.

Slice the bread into very thin pieces and serve with coffee.

*Prepare 1 day before baking.

Yield: 1 bread. Can be frozen.

Dough:
1 envelope yeast	¼ tsp. ground allspice
½ cup lukewarm water	1 cup chopped almonds
½ cup sugar	1 cup chopped hazelnuts
1¾ cups flour	½ cup diced candied citron
¼ tsp. cinnamon	½ cup diced orange peel
¼ tsp. ground cloves	1 cup pignolia nuts
¼ tsp. freshly grated nutmeg	Grated rind of 1 lemon

Frosting:
2 Tbs. water	Confectioners' sugar to sift
3 Tbs. sugar	over the bread
¼ tsp. cinnamon	2 Tbs. vegetable oil, not
¼ cup flour	olive oil

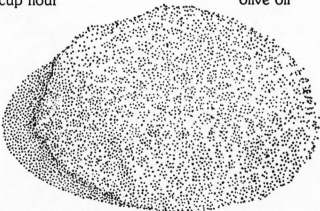

Dissolve the yeast in ¼ cup of the lukewarm water.

Measure the other ¼ cup of water and the ½ cup of sugar into a heavy saucepan. Heat over medium heat, stirring until the sugar is dissolved and you have a clear syrup. Let cool to lukewarm.

Add the syrup to the yeast mixture and stir in the flour with the spices. Add the nuts, the diced candied fruit and the grated lemon rind. Blend until you have a dough and place in a large buttered bowl. Cover with a towel and let stand for 2 hours. The dough will not rise much because of all the nuts and fruit.

Place the dough on a lightly floured work surface, knead for a few minutes and shape into a ball. Place the ball on an oiled baking sheet, cover with a towel and enclose in a plastic sheet. Let stand overnight. The plastic sheet will prevent a crust from forming.

The following day:

Preheat the oven to 375 degrees.

Make the frosting:

Heat the water with the sugar in a small heavy saucepan, until the sugar is dissolved and you have a clear syrup. Add the cinnamon and the oil and stir in the flour until you have a rather thick paste.

Spread the paste over the bread and bake for about 45 minutes or until light brown on top.

Let cool wrapped in a towel, and before serving sift a little confectioners' sugar over the bread.

JULEKAKE
Christmas Bread

This is a flavorful, sweet bread—especially good with coffee. Although it's a Christmas specialty in Norway, you can serve it all year round.

Yield: 2 large loaves. Can be frozen.

Dough:

1 envelope yeast
½ cup lukewarm water
1 tsp. sugar
1½ cups milk
1 stick butter
½ cup sugar
½ tsp. salt

2 eggs, slightly beaten
2 Tbs. crushed cardamom
   seeds
6½ to 7 cups flour
2 cups raisins
½ cup diced candied citron

Glaze:

Confectioners' sugar stirred
   with a little water

Preheat the oven to 375 degrees.

Proof the yeast in the lukewarm water with the teaspoon of sugar.

Scald the milk, add the butter and stir until melted. Let stand until lukewarm, then add this mixture to the yeast sponge. Add the half cup of sugar, salt, eggs and cardamom, and stir until blended. Measure in the flour, cup by cup, until you have a dough stiff enough to knead.

Stir in the raisins and the chopped citron.

Turn the dough out onto a lightly floured work surface and knead until shiny.

Place in a large buttered bowl, cover with a towel and let stand in a warm place to rise approximately 1 hour or until doubled in bulk.

Take the dough out and punch down a couple of times. Divide into 2 equal pieces and shape into loaves which you will place in 2 large (9" by 5") loaf pans that have been buttered.

Cover with a towel and let rise until doubled in size, about 45 minutes.

Then bake in the oven for about 35 minutes or until light brown and the loaves sound hollow when tapped with your finger.

Cool in the baking pans. When completely cool, take the loaves out onto a piece of wax paper and spread the glaze on top.

VANILJBOLLER
Vanilla Buns

Plain buns with a lovely surprise inside—vanilla custard.
The buns are very good with coffee as well as tea.

Yield: 24 buns. Do not freeze.

Dough:
1 envelope yeast	2 cups milk
¼ cup lukewarm water	1 egg, slightly beaten
3 Tbs. sugar	1 tsp. salt
2 Tbs. butter	About 5½ cups flour

Filling:
¾ cup milk	4 egg yolks
¼ cup sugar	1 tsp. vanilla

Preheat the oven to 375 degrees.

Proof the yeast in the water with the sugar.

Melt the butter and add the milk, heating until lukewarm. Add to the yeast sponge.

Stir in the egg, salt and flour and blend until you have a rather soft dough.

Turn the dough out onto a lightly floured work surface and knead

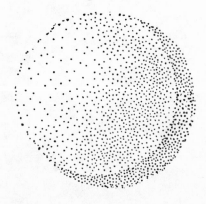

until elastic and not sticky, adding more flour if necessary.

Now place the dough in a large buttered bowl, cover with a towel and let rise for about 1 hour or until doubled in bulk.

Meanwhile make the custard filling:

Scald the milk. Beat the sugar with the egg yolks; pour a little of the milk into the eggs and stir. With the heat turned off, add the egg mixture to the milk. Stir over very low heat until the custard thickens, then immediately turn off the heat so that the custard doesn't curdle. After the custard has cooled, stir in the vanilla and let cool completely.

After the dough has doubled in size, take it out and knead for a few minutes. Divide into 2 or 3 pieces for easier handling and, with a rolling pin, roll each piece to a ⅓" thickness.

With a 2½" biscuit cutter, cut out rounds. Place about 1 teaspoon of custard on the middle of half the rounds. Take the remaining rounds and place on top, pinching the edges together to enclose the filling.

Place the filled buns on buttered baking sheets and cover with a towel.

Let rise about 35 to 45 minutes until doubled in size. Then bake until light brown, about 25 to 30 minutes.

Cool wrapped in a towel.

BREADS OF THE WORLD

WALNUT AND POPPY-SEED BREAD

Actually a coffee cake. It's very light and the filling is unusual and delicious.

Yield: 2 coffee cakes. Can be frozen.

Dough:
1 envelope yeast	⅓ cup sugar
¼ cup lukewarm water	1½ tsps. salt
⅔ cup milk	2 eggs
¼ stick butter	4 cups flour

Filling:
½ cup heavy cream	2 Tbs. flour
¼ cup sugar	¾ cup poppy seeds
¼ cup honey	1½ cups chopped walnuts

Preheat the oven to 375 degrees.

Dissolve the yeast in the lukewarm water.

Scald the milk and add the butter, sugar and salt. Pour into a large mixing bowl and let cool to lukewarm.

Add the eggs and the yeast mixture to the milk-and-butter mixture and stir in the flour, a little at a time, until you have a dough that you can knead.

Place the dough on a lightly floured work surface and knead for a couple of minutes, then place in a large buttered bowl. Cover with a towel and let stand in a warm place for about 1 hour or until doubled in bulk.

Meanwhile, in a heavy saucepan, measure in the heavy cream, sugar, honey, flour, poppy seeds and chopped walnuts. Bring to boil over medium heat, stirring all the time. Set aside to cool.

Now take out the dough, punch it down and knead for a couple of minutes. Divide into 2 equal pieces and, with a rolling pin, roll each piece out into a rectangle, about ¼″ thick.

Divide the nut filling and spread it evenly over each rectangle. Roll up the dough—like a jelly roll—and place the 2 rolls on 2 buttered baking sheets.

Cover and let rise for about 35 minutes, or until doubled in size. Then bake until golden brown, about 40 to 45 minutes.

Cool on a rack.

BREADS OF THE WORLD

MASSA SOVADA
Easter Bread

In the Christian tradition, the egg symbolizes continuity, fertility and the Resurrection; it is a lovely symbol. Place a hard-boiled egg on top of this bread before you bake and it might become a tradition in your home, too.

Yield: 2 round loaves. Can be frozen.

1 envelope yeast	4 eggs, slightly beaten
¼ cup lukewarm water	Grated rind and juice of 1
1 tsp. sugar	lemon
½ cup milk	5 to 5½ cups flour
1 stick butter	2 hard-boiled eggs in their
¾ cup sugar	shells
1 tsp. salt	

Preheat the oven to 400 degrees.

Proof the yeast in the lukewarm water with the teaspoon of sugar.

Scald the milk, add the butter, and let stand until the butter is melted and the mixture has become lukewarm. Add to the yeast sponge.

Add the sugar, salt and stir in the eggs and the lemon juice and rind. Stir in the flour, cup by cup, until you have a smooth dough.

Place the dough on a lightly floured work surface and knead until shiny.

Place the dough in a large buttered bowl, cover with a towel and let stand in a warm place to rise for about 2 hours.

Take the dough out and punch it down a couple of times. Cut off a piece of dough about the size of an orange and set that aside for decoration.

Divide the rest of the dough into 2 equal pieces, shape into 2 round loaves and place in 2 buttered 9" round baking pans.

Cover with a towel and let stand in a warm place until doubled in size, about 35 to 45 minutes.

Now place an egg in the middle of each bread, press down slightly so that it will stay in place. Divide the small piece of dough that you have set aside into four pieces. Roll into ropes about 9″ long and make a cross over each egg.

Bake in the oven until golden brown, about 30 to 35 minutes.

Cool on a rack.

PORTUGUESE SWEET BREAD

Sweet bread is good toasted for breakfast, but I like it even better plain with a glass of milk. Especially at night, it's wonderfully relaxing and seems to induce sleep.

Yield: 2 large round loaves. Can be frozen.

2 envelopes yeast
½ cup lukewarm water
1 tsp. sugar
1 cup milk
1 stick butter

1 cup sugar
1 tsp. salt
4 eggs
About 8 cups flour

Preheat the oven to 375 degrees.

Proof the yeast in the lukewarm water with the teaspoon of sugar.

Scald the milk, add the butter and sugar, stir and let dissolve. Let this mixture cool to lukewarm, then add to the yeast sponge. In a separate bowl, beat the eggs until frothy and add them to the yeast mixture as well.

Stir in the flour, cup by cup, until you have a dough that is soft but still firm enough to knead.

Turn the dough out onto a lightly floured work surface, knead for a few minutes, then place the dough in a large buttered bowl. Cover with a towel and let rise in a warm place for about 1 hour or until doubled in bulk.

Take the dough out, knead for a few minutes, and let it rest uncovered for about 15 minutes.

Punch the dough down and divide into 2 equal pieces. Shape these into 2 round loaves and place them in 2 buttered 9" pie forms. Cover with a towel and let rise for about 1 hour, or until doubled in size.

Bake in the oven until light brown and the loaves sound hollow when tapped with your finger, about 40 to 45 minutes.

Cool on a rack.

KULICH

Such a rich and festive holiday coffee cake! I bake this in two 2-pound coffee cans. You can do the same or use something similar.

When slicing, cut from the top in round pieces, but reserve the very top of the cake and replace to prevent the cake from drying.

Yield: 2 coffee cakes. Can be frozen.

1 envelope yeast
½ cup lukewarm water
¾ cup sugar
1½ sticks butter
1 cup milk
½ tsp. salt
5 egg yolks
About 6 cups flour
½ tsp. freshly grated nutmeg

1 cup golden raisins
½ cup candied lemon peel
½ cup candied orange peel
½ cup glazed cherries
Grated rind of 1 lemon
Butter and bread crumbs for
    coating the inside of the
    forms

Preheat the oven to 375 degrees.

Proof the yeast with the lukewarm water and the sugar.

Melt the butter over low heat, add the milk and the salt.

In a large mixing bowl blend together the yeast sponge and the cooled butter-milk-and-salt mixture.

Add the yolks, stirring to blend. Add the flour a little at a time, stirring with a wooden spoon until you have a fairly loose dough. Add the grated nutmeg.

In a separate bowl put the raisins, peel, cherries and grated lemon rind. Stir in a tablespoon of flour so that the fruits and peel won't stick together. Add the fruits to the dough and blend well.

Now turn the dough out onto a lightly floured work surface and knead for as long as you can—the longer the better.

Place the dough in a large buttered bowl, cover with a towel and let rise in a warm place until doubled in bulk.

This can take from 1 to 2 hours.

After the dough has risen, take it out again, knead for a couple of minutes and divide into 2 equal pieces.

Place in the 2 coffee cans or similar forms, which have been well buttered and sprinkled with bread crumbs.

Cover with a towel and let rise again for about 45 minutes.

Bake in the oven until the tops are golden and a cake tester comes out clean, about 45 to 50 minutes. If the tops brown too quickly, cover with a piece of foil.

Let cool in the forms until lukewarm, then remove and continue to cool wrapped in a towel.

UKRAINIAN COFFEE BREAD

A braided, festive-looking coffee cake. This is easy to make and goes very well with coffee or tea.

Yield: 1 large coffee bread. Can be frozen.

Dough:
1 envelope yeast	½ tsp. salt
¼ cup lukewarm water	1 tsp. vanilla extract
¼ cup soft butter	Grated peel of 1 lemon
½ cup sugar	3 to 4 cups flour
2 eggs	⅓ cup scalded milk, cooled
2 egg yolks	to lukewarm

Filling:
¼ cup sugar	¼ cup chopped walnuts
½ cup raisins	1 egg to brush the top

Preheat the oven to 400 degrees.

Dissolve the yeast in the lukewarm water.

In a large bowl cream the butter with the sugar until it is light and fluffy. Beat in the eggs and the yolks, 1 at a time, beating hard after each addition. Add the salt, vanilla and grated lemon peel. Add the yeast mixture and the flour; then add the milk, beating until shiny.

Place the dough in a large buttered bowl, cover and let rise in a warm place for about 1 hour or until doubled in bulk.

Place the dough on a lightly floured surface, punch it down a couple of times, and divide into 3 equal parts. Let it rest for a few minutes.

Meanwhile blend together the sugar, raisins and chopped walnuts and set aside.

Take 1 piece of dough, and with a rolling pin roll it out to an oblong shape, about 12″ long. Take ⅓ of the raisin-nut mixture and sprinkle it down the middle of the dough. Then fold each side to the center, covering the raisins and nuts, and pinch the ends together. Do the same with the other 2 pieces of dough.

Now, twist these 3 oblong pieces of dough together into a braid and place in a well-buttered (9″ by 5″) loaf pan.

Cover and let rise in a warm place for about 30 minutes.

Brush the top with the beaten egg and bake for about 25 minutes or until nicely brown on top. Cool wrapped in a towel.

BLÅBÄRSKAKA
Blueberry Cake

This is an old-fashioned cake, or bread, which to me, served with a glass of ice-cold milk, always means summer.

Nowadays, when either fresh or frozen blueberries can be had all year round, you can make this cake for all seasons.

Surprisingly enough, blueberry cake is made with rye flour and wheat flour.

It is delicious when eaten warm, but cold it is very good, too.

Yield: 1 large cake.

1 envelope yeast	2 cups rye flour
1 cup lukewarm milk	2 cups all-purpose flour
½ tsp. sugar	2 pints blueberries, fresh or
2 Tbs. melted butter	frozen
½ tsp. salt	½ cup to 1 cup sugar to
½ tsp. crushed fennel	sprinkle on top

Preheat the oven to 375 degrees.

Proof the yeast in the lukewarm milk with the sugar. Add the melted butter to the yeast sponge; then the salt, crushed fennel, rye flour and about 1 cup of the all-purpose flour. Blend the dough and turn it out onto a lightly floured work surface. Knead until shiny, adding more all-purpose flour if the dough seems too sticky.

Place the dough in a large buttered bowl, cover with a towel and let rise in a warm, draft-free place for about 1 hour or until doubled in bulk.

Now knead the dough for about 10 minutes, adding a little more flour if it is too soft. With a rolling pin, roll the dough into a rectangle large enough to fit a buttered (17″ by 11″) baking pan with the edges sticking out a little over the rim.

Pour the blueberries on top of the dough and spread them out evenly.

Cover with a towel and let rise for 45 minutes. Now sprinkle the sugar on top of the blueberries and bake about 30 to 35 minutes or until the crust around the rim of the baking pan is a nice light brown.

Leave the cake in the pan to cool. You may want to sprinkle a little more sugar on top. Cut into squares and serve warm if possible, though you may freeze these.

BULLAR
Sweet Buns

No home in Sweden would ever be without these, and they must be homebaked. They are probably the first thing a little girl learns to make. Everybody has a special variation: some add almonds or hazelnuts to the filling; some alter the spices or add grated apple or grated lemon or orange rind.

But the buns always contain cardamom, freshly crushed to get the most exciting taste and fragrance out of this wonderful spice.

Fantastic when served warm with coffee or a glass of cold milk, but delicious cold too.

Yield: 30 buns. Can be frozen.

Dough:
    1 envelope yeast   ½ cup sugar
    ¼ cup lukewarm milk   1 tsp. salt
    1 tsp. sugar   3 eggs
    1¾ cups milk   2 tsps. crushed cardamom
    1 stick butter   seeds

Filling:
    1 stick soft butter
    ½ cup sugar
    2 Tbs. cinnamon

Glaze:
    1 beaten egg for brushing
    Pearl sugar (coarse sugar) or
        granulated sugar to
        sprinkle on top

Preheat the oven to 400 degrees.

Proof the yeast in the ¼ cup lukewarm milk with the teaspoon of sugar.

Scald the rest of the milk, then add the stick of butter to melt. Cool to lukewarm.

In a large mixing bowl, blend together the yeast sponge with the milk-and-butter mixture. Add the sugar and salt. Stir in the eggs, 1 at a time, and the cardamom.

Add the flour, cup by cup. Blend and place the dough on a lightly floured work surface. Knead until shiny and elastic. If it sticks, knead in more flour.

Place the dough in a large buttered bowl, cover with a towel and let rise in a warm place for about 45 minutes to 1 hour or until the dough has doubled in bulk.

Take the dough out onto your work surface, knead a couple of times and divide into 3 pieces.

With a rolling pin, roll each piece into a rectangle that is about 10″ long and ¼″ thick.

Spread ⅓ of the butter on top of each piece of dough. Likewise sprinkle ⅓ of the sugar and ⅓ of the cinnamon as evenly as you can.

Fold the dough lengthwise into thirds and, with a knife, cut into slices that are 1½″ wide. Now halve each slice lengthwise almost completely but leave attached at the top. Pull the slits gently until elongated but still not breaking and twist them so that they look like a piece of rope; then twirl into a fancy shape.

Place on buttered baking sheets. Do the same with the rest of the dough.

Cover with a towel and let stand in a warm place to rise for about 25 minutes. Brush with the beaten egg and sprinkle with sugar.

Bake until golden brown, about 20 to 25 minutes. Cool wrapped in a towel.

FETTISDAGSBULLAR
Lenten Buns

Very rich buns that are usually served for lunch every Tuesday during Lent. To serve them correctly, place the bun in a soup bowl, pour warm milk around it and eat with a soup spoon.

It is a very filling dish, so you need only serve a salad beforehand to complete your meal.

Yield: 16 to 18 buns. Can be frozen unfilled.

1 envelope yeast
½ cup lukewarm milk
1 tsp. sugar
1½ cups light cream
½ stick butter
3 egg yolks
¼ cup sugar

½ tsp. salt
About 5½ cups flour
1 package imported almond
   paste (7 oz.)
1½ cups heavy cream
Confectioners' sugar

Preheat the oven to 400 degrees.

Proof the yeast in the lukewarm milk with the teaspoon of sugar.

Scald the light cream and add the butter to melt. Then cool to lukewarm.

Blend the yeast sponge with the cream-and-butter and stir in the egg yolks, sugar, salt and flour, cup by cup. Blend well.

Turn the dough out onto a lightly floured work surface and knead until shiny and smooth. Add a little more flour if the dough is sticky, but it should be a rather soft dough.

Now place the dough in a large buttered bowl, cover with a towel and let stand in a warm place to rise until doubled in bulk. This should take about 1 hour.

After the dough has doubled, take it out and knead for a couple of minutes.

Cut off pieces the size of tangerines and roll into balls.

Place these on lightly buttered baking sheets, not too close together.

Cover with a towel and let rise until doubled in size, about 35 to 45 minutes.

Bake in the oven about 25 to 30 minutes or until light brown. Cool wrapped in a towel.

After the buns have cooled, cut a triangle, about 1½" on each side, off the top and set aside. Scoop out about 1 teaspoonful of the inside of each bun and place the scooped out bread in a bowl. Add the almond paste and about 3 tablespoons of the heavy cream; with an electric mixer blend until smooth.

Fill each bun with some of the mixture.

Whip the rest of the heavy cream until stiff and put about 1 heaping tablespoon on top of the almond filling. Replace the little triangle that you previously cut off, like a little cap, on top and dust with confectioners' sugar.

KANELBROD
Cinnamon Bread

Delicious eaten as is, but this bread also makes wonderful toast.

Yield: 3 large breads. Can be frozen.

Dough:

1 envelope yeast	½ cup sugar
¼ cup lukewarm milk	1 tsp. salt
1 tsp. sugar	3 eggs
1¾ cups milk	6 to 7 cups flour
1 stick butter	

Filling:

1 stick soft butter	1 beaten egg for brushing
9 Tbs. sugar	the tops
9 Tbs. cinnamon	

Preheat the oven to 400 degrees.

Proof the yeast in the lukewarm milk with the 1 teaspoon of sugar.

Scald the rest of the milk, then add the stick of butter, allowing it to melt. Cool to lukewarm.

In a large mixing bowl, blend the yeast sponge with the milk-and-butter mixture. Add the sugar and salt. Stir in the eggs, 1 at a time, each slightly beaten. Add the flour, cup by cup, stirring until blended, and place the dough on a lightly floured work surface. Knead until shiny. If it sticks, knead in more flour.

Place the dough in a large buttered bowl, cover with a towel and let rise in a warm place for about 1 hour or until doubled in bulk.

Turn the dough out onto your work surface, knead for about 10 minutes, then divide into 3 equal pieces.

With a rolling pin roll each piece into a rectangle, about ¼" thick. Spread each rectangle with butter, sprinkle with sugar and cinnamon and roll, jelly-roll style.

Place the rolls in 3 large (9″ by 5″) buttered loaf pans.

Cover with a towel and let rise in a warm place for about 40 to 45 minutes.

Brush with the beaten egg and bake about 30 to 35 minutes or until light brown and the loaves sound hollow when tapped with your finger.

Cool wrapped in a towel.

KRYDDSKORPOR
Spicy Zwieback

Not really a pastry and not really a bread, something right in between. They keep forever in a cookie tin. Dunk them in coffee or milk as a snack.

The recipe is a very old and a very good one.

Yield: 100 zwiebacks.

1 envelope yeast	1 tsp. anise seeds
½ cup lukewarm milk	1 tsp. fennel seeds
½ cup sugar	½ tsp. salt
1½ cups milk	About 6 cups flour
1 stick butter	
1 piece pomerance (see page 19 for how to make)	

Preheat the oven to 400 degrees.

Proof the yeast in the ½ cup lukewarm milk with the sugar.

Scald the 1½ cups of milk and add the butter, pomerance, anise seeds and fennel seeds. Cool until lukewarm.

Pour the milk-and-butter mixture into the blender and blend until the pomerance and the seeds are crushed; add to the yeast sponge.

Add the salt and the flour, cup by cup, until you have a rather stiff dough.

Place the dough in a large buttered bowl, cover with a towel and let stand in a warm place to rise until doubled in bulk. This should take about 1 hour.

After the dough has doubled in bulk, turn it out onto your work surface and knead a couple of minutes. Then divide into 4 pieces of equal size.

Shape each piece of dough into a roll, about 12″ long, and place on buttered baking sheets, 2 rolls to a sheet.

Cover with a towel and let stand in a warm place to rise for 20 minutes.

Bake in the oven about 20 to 25 minutes or until light brown. Place on a rack to cool.

When completely cool, cut into slices about ⅓″ wide. Place the slices close together on an unbuttered baking sheet and put in the oven at 450 degrees to toast until light brown, about 20 to 25 minutes. Turn down the heat to 150 degrees (or turn the heat off completely if your oven doesn't go that low) and let the zwieback dry completely. This will take about 1 hour or until they feel absolutely dry and not spongy.

Store in a cookie tin in a dry place.

LUSSEKATTER
St. Lucia's Cats

In Sweden on the 13th of December, Saint Lucia is celebrated with festivities that start at the crack of dawn and last all day. Beautiful young girls dress in white and wear wreaths on their heads, made from the branches of lingonberry bushes and topped with lighted candles. They visit homes, factories, offices and hospitals, serving coffee with *Lussekatter* and large gingerbread cookies.

Lussekatter are made in different ancient curlicued shapes and are pretty as well as delicious to eat.

Yield: 20 buns. Can be frozen.

1 envelope yeast	1½ sticks melted and cooled
2 cups lukewarm milk	butter
¾ cup sugar	5½ to 6 cups flour
½ to 1 tsp. powdered	1 beaten egg for brushing
saffron, according to	¾ cup raisins for decoration
taste	
½ tsp. salt	

Preheat the oven to 400 degrees.

Dissolve the yeast in the lukewarm milk, add the sugar, saffron and salt, and stir. Add the melted butter and stir in the flour, a cup at a time, but save about ½ cup for dusting your work surface.

Turn the dough out onto your floured work surface and knead until all the flour is incorporated and the dough is shiny and not sticky but still rather soft.

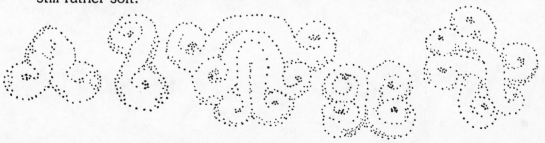

Place the dough in a large buttered bowl, cover with a towel and let rise in a warm place for about 1 hour or until doubled in bulk.

Return the dough to your work surface, knead for about 10 minutes and divide into 30 pieces of equal size.

Roll each piece out into a rope about ¾″ thick and shape into fanciful buns (see illustrations). Place the buns on lightly buttered baking sheets (not too close together) and cover with a towel.

Let rise until doubled in bulk, about 25 to 30 minutes, then poke in raisins (where shown) and brush with the egg. Bake until golden, about 20 to 25 minutes.

Cool wrapped in a towel.

SAFFRON CARDAMOM BRAID

A rich, delicious coffee cake, served at Christmastime.

Yield: 2 large braids. Can be frozen.

Dough:
1 envelope yeast	½ cup sugar
¼ cup lukewarm milk	1 tsp. salt
1 tsp. sugar	½ tsp. powdered saffron
1¾ cups milk	2 eggs
1 stick butter	About 6 cups flour

Filling:
¾ stick soft butter	1½ cups raisins
5 Tbs. sugar	1 beaten egg for brushing
1 Tbs. crushed cardamom seeds	

Preheat the oven to 400 degrees.

Proof the yeast in the lukewarm milk with the teaspoon of sugar.

Scald the rest of the milk, then add the stick of butter. Let melt and cool to lukewarm.

In a large mixing bowl, blend together the yeast sponge with the milk-and-butter mixture. Add the sugar, salt and saffron. Stir in the eggs, 1 at a time. Add the flour, cup by cup, blend and place the dough on a lightly floured work surface. Knead until shiny and elastic. If it sticks to your hands, knead in more flour.

Place the dough in a large buttered bowl, cover with a towel and let rise in a warm place for about 45 minutes to 1 hour or until doubled in bulk.

Turn the dough out onto your work surface, knead for a couple of minutes and divide into 2 equal pieces. Set 1 piece aside.

Divide the remaining piece of dough into 3 equal pieces and with a rolling pin roll into 3 rectangles, about 4" to 5" wide.

Divide the butter, sugar, cardamom and raisins into 2 equal portions and set aside half. Divide the remaining half among the 3 rectangles:

Spread the butter first, then sprinkle the sugar, cardamom and raisins on top and roll up the rectangles jelly-roll style, pinching the ends together so that the filling won't seep out when baking.

Place the 3 rolls next to each other, braid them together and place on a lightly buttered cookie sheet.

Take the remaining piece of dough, divide into 3 and proceed as above.

You now have 2 rather large braids, 1 on each cookie sheet.

Cover with a towel and let rise until doubled in size, about 35 to 45 minutes. Brush with the beaten egg and bake until golden brown, about 30 to 35 minutes.

Cool wrapped in a towel.

SHOKLADGIFFEL
Chocolate Crescent

A coffee cake for chocolate lovers.

Yield: 2 coffee cakes. Can be frozen.

Dough:

1 envelope yeast
¼ cup lukewarm milk
1 tsp. sugar
1¾ cups milk
1 stick butter

½ cup sugar
1 tsp. salt
3 eggs
6 to 7 cups flour

Filling:

1 cup sugar
⅓ cup cocoa
1 cup chopped hazelnuts

¼ tsp. cinnamon
½ cup water
1 beaten egg for brushing

Preheat the oven to 400 degrees.

Proof the yeast in the lukewarm milk with the teaspoon of sugar.

Scald the rest of the milk, then add the stick of butter. Let melt, then cool to lukewarm.

In a large mixing bowl, blend the yeast sponge with the milk-and-butter mixture. Add the sugar and salt. Stir in the eggs, 1 at a time, each slightly beaten. Add the flour, cup by cup, stir and place the dough on a lightly floured work surface. Knead until shiny. If it sticks, knead in more flour.

Place the dough in a large buttered bowl, cover with a towel and let rise in a warm place for about 45 minutes to 1 hour or until doubled in bulk.

Meanwhile, make the filling by making a spreadable paste of the sugar, cocoa, hazelnuts, cinnamon and water. Set aside.

Return the dough to the work surface, knead for a few minutes and divide into 2 equal pieces.

With a rolling pin, roll each piece into a rectangle about ¼" thick and 18" long. Spread the chocolate paste down the center of each piece of dough, fold the pieces lengthwise, pinching the edges together. Shape into a crescent and place on buttered baking sheets.

Cover with a towel and let rise in a warm place for 40 minutes. Brush the crescents with the beaten egg and bake until golden brown, about 25 to 30 minutes. Cool on a rack.

SLOTTSKRINGLOR
Castle Pretzels

There is something very comforting about the shape of a pretzel, and these are especially lovely because they are sprinkled with sugar before baking. They exude a wonderful fragrance while in the oven, and if you serve them warm with some piping hot chocolate on a chilly day, your reputation as a considerate person, as well as a good baker, will be made.

Yield: 36 pretzels. Can be frozen.

1 cup soft butter
¼ cup sugar
½ cup lukewarm milk
2 to 2½ cups flour

1 envelope yeast
1 cup pearl sugar (coarse
    sugar) or granulated
    sugar to sprinkle on top

Preheat the oven to 350 degrees.

In a large bowl with an electric mixer, beat the butter and the sugar until pale and fluffy. Add the lukewarm milk, about 2 cups of the flour and the yeast, and blend well.

Add some more of the flour if the dough seems too soft to handle.

Dust your work surface with the rest of the flour and knead the soft dough for a few minutes, incorporating just enough flour so the dough is still soft but not sticky. Do not let the dough rise but immediately roll it out into about 36 lengths, the thickness of your finger, and shape into pretzels.

Dip these in the coarse sugar, pressing lightly so that the sugar will stick; or sprinkle the sugar on top and press to make it stick.

Place the pretzels on buttered baking sheets. Cover with a towel and let rise in a warm place for about 20 to 30 minutes.

Don't let them rise too much. They should not double in size.

Bake in the oven until pale golden, about 30 to 35 minutes.

Cool on a rack. Serve warm or cold.

BIRNENWECKEN
Pear Bread

Do not serve this bread fresh. It tastes best when it is a few days old. You might experiment by using mixed dried fruit instead of just dried pears.

Yield: 1 large bread. Can be frozen.

Dough:

    1 envelope yeast
    ¼ cup lukewarm water
    ½ cup sugar
    ½ cup milk

    ½ stick butter
    1 tsp. salt
    1 egg, slightly beaten
    4 to 4½ cups flour

Filling:

    1 pound dried pears (about
        4 cups)
    1 cup raisins
    ½ cup chopped walnuts
    Grated rind and juice of 1
        lemon

    ½ tsp. nutmeg
    ½ tsp. cinnamon
    ¾ cup sugar
    ½ cup kirsch

Preheat the oven to 350 degrees.

Proof the yeast in the lukewarm water with the sugar.

Scald the milk and stir in the butter to melt. Let stand until lukewarm.

Add the milk-and-butter to the yeast sponge; then add the salt and the egg and stir in the flour, cup by cup.

Place the dough on a lightly floured work surface and knead until elastic and smooth but still soft. Place the dough in a large buttered bowl, cover with a towel and let stand in a warm place for about 1 hour or until doubled in bulk.

Meanwhile, place the dried pears in a saucepan, cover with water and bring to a boil; then lower the heat and simmer for about 20 minutes or until the pears are softened.

Pour the water off and put the pears and the raisins through the coarse blade on a meat grinder, or blend in a blender.

Stir in the walnuts, grated lemon rind and juice, the spices, sugar and kirsch. Stir until you have a smooth paste.

Now, with a rolling pin, roll out the dough on your work surface until it is about 18″ long on each side, forming a square. Spread the fruit paste as evenly as you can on top and roll up, jelly-roll fashion.

Place the roll on a buttered baking sheet, cover with a towel and let stand in a warm place for about 1 hour or until doubled in size. Bake until golden, about 45 to 50 minutes. Cool on a rack. Wait at least 1 day before slicing.

BOURBON STICKY BUNS

These are sticky and sweet and delicious! Especially if you serve them warm.

Yield: 18 to 20 buns. Can be frozen.

1 envelope yeast
1½ cups milk, scalded and
    cooled to lukewarm
2 Tbs. sugar
½ tsp. salt
1 egg yolk

4 cups flour
½ cup bourbon
2 cups light brown sugar
1 cup whole pecans
½ stick soft butter
2 tsps. cinnamon

Preheat the oven to 375 degrees.

Proof the yeast in the lukewarm milk with the sugar.

Add the salt, egg yolk and flour to the yeast sponge, mixing together. Turn the dough out onto a lightly floured work surface and knead until smooth and shiny.

Place the dough in a large buttered bowl, cover with a towel and let rise for about 1 hour or until doubled in bulk.

Meanwhile butter muffin tins, and measure into each: 1 teaspoon of bourbon, 1 heaping tablespoon of light brown sugar and 3 or more whole pecans.

Now turn the dough out on your work surface, knead a couple of minutes and divide into 2 pieces.

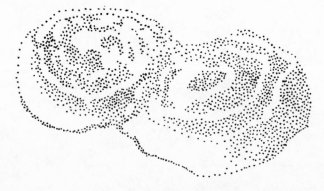

With a rolling pin, roll each piece into a rectangle and spread with the soft butter. Sprinkle the remainder of the light brown sugar, any leftover bourbon and the cinnamon on top.

Now roll the dough up, jelly-roll style, and cut each roll into 9 or 10 pieces of equal size. Place these in the prepared muffin tins.

Cover with a towel and let stand in a warm place to rise about 35 to 45 minutes until doubled in size. Then bake until golden brown, about 25 to 30 minutes.

Remove the buns at once from the muffin tins and let cool slightly before serving.

CINNAMON ROLLS

Quite irresistible! These rolls smell, taste and look beautiful.
Serve with breakfast or perhaps with afternoon coffee or tea.

Yield: 30 rolls. Can be frozen.

Dough:
1 envelope yeast
¼ cup lukewarm milk
1 tsp. sugar
1¾ cups milk
½ stick butter

¼ cup sugar
1 tsp. salt
3 eggs
6 to 7 cups flour

Filling:
½ stick melted butter
½ cup sugar
3 to 4 Tbs. cinnamon

Preheat the oven to 400 degrees.

Proof the yeast in the lukewarm milk with the teaspoon of sugar.
Scald the rest of the milk, then add the butter to melt. Cool to lukewarm.
In a large mixing bowl, blend the yeast sponge with the milk-and-butter mixture. Add the sugar and salt. Stir in the eggs, one at a time. Add the flour, cup by cup, blend and place the dough on a lightly floured work surface. Knead until shiny and elastic. If it sticks, knead in more flour.
Place the dough in a large buttered bowl, cover with a towel and let rise in a warm place for about 45 minutes to 1 hour or until doubled in bulk.
Turn the dough out onto your work surface, knead a couple of times and divide into 3 parts for easier handling.
With a rolling pin, roll each piece into a rectangle that is about ¼" thick and 9" wide. Brush each rectangle with the melted butter. Then

sprinkle with the sugar and cinnamon, divided evenly between the 3 rectangles of dough.

Roll up tightly, jelly-roll fashion, and cut into pieces that are about 1½″ wide. Place these in muffin tins that have been brushed with melted butter. Cover with a towel and let stand in a warm place to rise until doubled in size, about 35 to 45 minutes.

Brush the tops with some additional melted butter before you put them in the oven.

Bake until golden brown, about 20 to 25 minutes. Cool wrapped in a towel.

8
SOURDOUGH BREADS

SOURDOUGH STARTER

I am not that fond of making bread the sourdough way, but I do keep a starter at home. It requires some doing, but for those of you who love the taste of sourdough bread and who might like the challenge of making and maintaining the starter, here's a foolproof method.

My recipe for starter is perhaps cheating a bit, since I use an envelope of dry yeast. However, the bread made from it is good, indeed.

Yield: 4 cups starter.

2 cups warm water
3 cups flour
2 tsps. salt
2 tsps. sugar

1 envelope yeast
1½ cups grated, raw
   potatoes

Mix the warm water with the flour, salt, sugar, yeast and grated potatoes and blend well. Pour into a fairly large container made of glass or, better still, an earthenware bowl. Do not use plastic or metal.

Put the bowl in a warm place for 24 hours, uncovered. Then stir down well, cover with a sheet of plastic and let stand in a warm place for 3 to 4 more days. Stir a couple of times each day.

The starter should now look a bit foamy and start to smell. Pour it into a glass jar with a lid and store in the refrigerator.

You can begin to use the starter when a layer of clear liquid appears on top.

The night before you want to bake, take the starter out of the refrigerator, pour it into a bowl (not plastic or metal) and stir in 1½ cups flour and 1½ cups cold water. Stir until well blended and smooth, cover with a piece of plastic and set in a warm place overnight.

The next morning stir the starter again and pour off 2 cups into your glass jar. Put this back into the refrigerator for next time. The remaining 2 cups of starter are what you will use for your immediate baking.

SOURDOUGH FRENCH BREAD

If you don't like your sourdough bread quite as sour, adjust the recipe and use 1 cup starter and 2 cups water. The following version is my favorite.

Yield: 2 large or 3 or 4 small loaves. Can be frozen.

1 envelope yeast	1 Tbs. salt
1 cup lukewarm water	5½ to 6 cups flour
2 cups sourdough starter	

Preheat the oven to 450 degrees.

Dissolve the yeast in the lukewarm water, then add the sourdough starter, salt and flour, and mix until you have a rather stiff dough. Then turn the dough out onto a lightly floured work surface and knead for about 10 minutes to get a nice, shiny dough.

Place the dough in a large buttered bowl and rotate the dough so that all sides get covered with the butter. Cover with a towel and let stand in a warm place to rise until doubled in bulk, about 1½ hours.

Take the dough out again and knead for a couple of minutes. Divide into 2 or more parts. If you have French bread forms shape the dough into ropes and place in the lightly buttered forms. If you are going to use a baking sheet, roll each piece of dough out with a rolling pin into a rectangle. Then roll up, jelly-roll fashion, and place on the buttered baking sheet.

Let stand in a warm draft-free place, uncovered, to rise until doubled in size, about 30 to 45 minutes.

Before you place the breads in the oven, make about 4 to 5 slashes diagonally across the tops of the loaves with a razor blade.

Place the loaves in the hot oven and bake for 15 minutes. Then reduce the heat to 375 degrees and continue to bake for about another 25 minutes or until the loaves are nicely brown and sound hollow when tapped with your finger.

Cool uncovered on a rack.

SCHWARZWALDER ROGGEN BROT
Black Forest Rye Bread

A dark, hearty bread that I like thickly sliced, spread with mustard and covered with smoked ham, maybe *Bauernschinke* if you can get it. Drink beer with your big sandwich and enjoy!

Yield: 2 small loaves. Can be frozen.

1 envelope yeast	1 Tbs. salt
½ cup lukewarm water	1 Tbs. caraway seeds
1 tsp. sugar	3 cups coarse rye flour (rye
1 cup sourdough starter	meal)
½ cup lard	2 cups whole-wheat flour
1 cup milk	

Preheat the oven to 400 degrees.

Proof the yeast in the lukewarm water with the sugar. Add the sourdough starter to the yeast sponge. Melt the lard, pour the milk over it and let stand until lukewarm. Then add to the yeast mixture.

Measure in the salt, caraway seeds and the coarse rye flour. Then add the whole-wheat flour.

Place the dough on a lightly floured work surface and knead until smooth and elastic; then place in a large buttered bowl, cover with a towel and let stand in a warm place to rise for about 1½ hours or until doubled in bulk.

Take the dough out onto your work surface and punch it down a couple of times; divide into 2 equal pieces, and knead these for a couple of minutes. Then place into 2 small (8″ by 4″) buttered loaf pans, cover with a towel and let rise until doubled in size, about 30 to 45 minutes.

Bake in the oven until the tops are brown and the loaves sound hollow when tapped with your finger, about 35 to 40 minutes.

Cool on a rack.

BALTIC RYE BREAD

The recipe for this bread was developed by a Lithuanian friend who, after many trials and errors, found that he had created a bread that tasted like the one on which he grew up. It slices beautifully and is spectacular with lots of butter and cheese.

Yield: 2 large loaves. Can be frozen.

1 envelope yeast
½ cup lukewarm water
1 tsp. sugar
2 cups leftover coffee
1 square (1 oz.) semisweet
   chocolate
¼ cup molasses

2 cups sourdough starter
2 Tbs. caraway seeds
2 Tbs. salt
2 cups 100% bran cereal
   that's been ground in a
   blender
About 6 cups rye flour

Preheat the oven to 375 degrees.

Proof the yeast in the lukewarm water with the sugar.

Bring the coffee to a boil, turn off the heat, and stir in the chocolate to let it melt. Add the molasses and stir again. Let cool until lukewarm.

Blend together the yeast mixture, the coffee mixture and the sourdough starter. Add the caraway seeds, salt, ground bran cereal and stir in the flour, cup by cup.

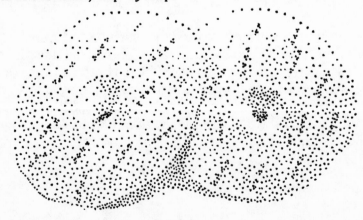

When you have a dough that you can knead, place it on a lightly floured (all-purpose flour) work surface, kneading until elastic and shiny.

Place in a large buttered bowl, cover with a towel and let stand in a warm place to rise until doubled in bulk. This should take about 1 to 1½ hours.

Take the dough out again and punch down a couple of times. Divide into 2 equal pieces, shape these into two round loaves and place on a buttered baking sheet. Cover with a towel and let stand in a warm place for about 1 hour or until doubled in size.

Bake about 50 to 55 minutes or until brown and the breads sound hollow when tapped with your finger. Cool the breads wrapped in a towel.

MEDELTIDA BRÖD
Bread from the Middle Ages

The first grains to be cultivated in Scandinavia were wheat and barley. In the beginning, about 2000 B.C., no leavening was used in the preparation of grain. A porridge was made instead, very often including pieces of fish or meat. Almost three thousand years later, sourdough bread became popular.

This recipe has an interesting sweet-sour flavor and has been handed down in my family since the 13th century with a few slight changes.

Yield: 2 large round loaves. Can be frozen.

1 envelope yeast	½ stick melted butter or ¼
½ cup lukewarm water	cup of shortening
2 cups sourdough starter	2 cups barley flour
1 tsp. salt	2 cups whole-wheat flour
⅓ cup honey	1 cup all-purpose flour

Preheat the oven to 375 degrees.

Dissolve the yeast in the lukewarm water. Add the sourdough starter, salt, honey and shortening. Stir until well blended. Add the barley flour, whole-wheat flour, all-purpose flour and blend.

Turn the dough out onto a lightly floured work surface and knead for a couple of minutes. Place the dough in a large buttered bowl, cover with a towel and let stand in a warm place to rise for about 1 hour or until doubled in bulk.

Punch the dough down a couple of times and knead for a couple of minutes. Divide the dough into 2 equal pieces and shape these into round balls. Place on a lightly buttered baking sheet, cover with a towel and let stand until doubled in size. This should take about 40 to 45 minutes.

Bake for about 30 minutes or until nicely brown and the loaves sound hollow when tapped with your finger.

Cool wrapped in a towel.

PLAIN WHITE SOURDOUGH BREAD

Very popular in the Old West, this basic sourdough bread can be used for making loaves or rolls. It makes an excellent sandwich base, since it slices beautifully and has a nice subtle taste. If you add a little extra sugar, you can use it as a base for various kinds of coffee cakes.

Yield: 3 small loaves or 24 rolls. Can be frozen.

1 envelope yeast	4 Tbs. melted butter
½ cup lukewarm water	2 Tbs. salt
4 Tbs. sugar	About 7 cups flour
2 cups sourdough starter	1 beaten egg for brushing
2 cups lukewarm milk	the tops

Preheat the oven to 375 degrees.
Proof the yeast in the lukewarm water with the sugar. Add the starter, milk, melted butter and salt, and stir in the flour, cup by cup, until you have a dough that you can knead.

Turn it out onto a lightly floured work surface and knead until elastic and not sticky. Add some flour if necessary.

Place the dough in a large buttered bowl, cover with a towel, and let stand in a warm place to rise for about 1 hour or until doubled in bulk.

Take the dough out again, punch it down a couple of times and, if you are making loaves, divide into 3 equal pieces. Shape these into loaves and place in 3 small (8" by 4") loaf pans that have been buttered.

Cover with a towel and let stand until doubled in size, about 45 minutes. Then brush with the beaten egg and place in the oven.

Bake until beautifully golden and the breads sound hollow when tapped with your finger, about 50 to 55 minutes.

If you are making rolls, divide the dough into 24 equal pieces, place these in buttered muffin pans, cover with a towel and let rise until doubled in size. Brush with the beaten egg and bake until golden, about 30 minutes.

Cool the breads or rolls on a rack.

BREADS OF THE WORLD

SOURDOUGH BUTTER ROLLS

So buttery and soft, these rolls are particularly delicious served warm with butter and blackberry jam at afternoon tea.

Yield: 36 rolls. Can be frozen.

1 envelope yeast
½ cup lukewarm water
4 Tbs. sugar
2 cups sourdough starter
2 cups lukewarm milk

4 Tbs. melted butter
1 Tbs. salt
About 7 cups flour
1 stick melted butter to pour
    on top of the rolls

Preheat the oven to 400 degrees.

Proof the yeast in the lukewarm water with the sugar.

Add the starter, milk, 4 Tbs. melted butter and salt; stir in the flour, cup by cup, until you have a dough that you can knead.

Turn it out on a lightly floured work surface and knead until elastic and not sticky. Add some flour, if necessary, to get the right consistency.

Place the dough in a large buttered bowl, cover with a towel and let stand in a warm place to rise for about 1 hour, or until doubled in bulk.

Take the dough out again, punch it down a couple of times and divide into 36 equal pieces. Shape these into little buns; they do not have to be perfectly even. Place in buttered muffin pans, cover with a towel and let stand in a warm place to rise for about 35 to 40 minutes.

Pour a little of the melted butter on every roll and bake in the oven until light brown, about 20 to 25 minutes.

Serve warm if possible.

SOURDOUGH PANCAKES

These American pancakes are made with a sourdough starter, which lends a certain charming taste.

I like to make them with half whole-wheat and half all-purpose flour, but you can use only all-purpose flour if you like.

The sourdough flavor contrasts particularly well with the maple syrup.

Yield: About 24 pancakes. Can be frozen.

1 cup sourdough starter	1½ tsps. baking soda
2 Tbs. melted butter	1 cup whole-wheat flour
1 egg, slightly beaten	1 cup all-purpose flour
½ tsp. salt	1 cup milk

Blend all the ingredients together (do not overmix) and let stand for 30 minutes.

Heat a little butter in a preheated skillet and bake fairly small pancakes over medium heat, turning once so that both sides turn light brown.

Serve at once while hot.

9
SAVORY QUICK BREADS

BANNOCK

Bannock is the Indian forerunner of our North-American baking powder biscuits. I like them warm with butter and honey.

Yield: 2 small round cakes. Can be frozen.

3 cups flour
½ cup wheat germ
2 tsps. baking soda
½ tsp. cream of tartar
1 tsp. salt

¼ cup melted butter or
    bacon fat
2 Tbs. molasses
1¼ cups buttermilk

Preheat the oven to 375 degrees.

Blend the dry ingredients together. Stir the molasses and buttermilk into the melted butter or bacon fat and add to the flour mixture. Stir until blended, then knead for a few minutes on a lightly floured work surface. Divide into 2 equal pieces and shape into 2 cakes about 6" in diameter. Place these on a buttered baking sheet and bake until golden, for about 25 to 30 minutes.

Cool on a rack.

MARYLO VELASCO'S EMPANADAS CHILENAS
Chilean Turnover

These turnovers plus a bottle of red wine make for simple but tasty picnic fare. You can prepare the turnovers ahead of time and eat them either reheated or cold.

The recipe was given to me by one of my favorite people, a friend from Viña Del Mar in Chile.

Yield: 20 empanadas. Can be frozen.

Dough:

5 cups flour	2 egg yolks, slightly beaten
2 tsps. baking powder	1½ cups milk
1 tsp. salt	2 sticks butter

Filling:

1 lb. ground round STEAK	2 Tbs. crushed cumin seeds
1 cup beef broth (may be canned)	1½ tsps. salt
4 large onions, chopped	3 hard-boiled eggs
3 Tbs. butter	20 black olives, sliced
2 Tbs. paprika	1 beaten egg white for brushing

Preheat the oven to 400 degrees.

The filling should be cold when you make the turnovers, so you really should prepare it in advance, perhaps even a day ahead.

To make the filling:

Boil the meat in the broth until it is no longer pink, about 10 to 15 minutes.

Fry the onions in the butter until golden and stir in the paprika, cumin and salt.

Stir the onion mixture into the cooked meat and simmer for about 5 minutes; then set aside to cool.

To make the dough:

Place the flour in a large bowl with the baking powder and salt. Make a well in the center and add the egg yolks.

Scald the milk and add the butter to melt. Add this to the flour and blend well. Turn out onto a lightly floured work surface and knead until smooth.

Let the dough rest, covered with a towel, for 20 minutes.

Now take the dough and divide into 3 or 4 pieces for easier handling, and with a rolling pin roll each piece out until it is very thin but still holds together.

With a pastry wheel cut into 5″ squares. Place a heaping tablespoon of the meat filling on each square, put a few slices of hard-boiled egg and sliced olives on top and close the dough like an envelope, over the filling. Moisten the edges with a little bit of water to make them stick together. Place on a lightly buttered baking sheet, brush with the beaten egg white and bake until golden brown, about 15 to 20 minutes.

FLADBRØD
Flat Oatmeal Bread

Fladbrød is almost like a pancake. It's easy to make and delightful for breakfast with butter and honey; or you might try serving it with maple syrup or jam or even rolled up around a creamy filling.

Yield: 8 thin breads. Can be frozen.

1½ cups buttermilk
1 stick melted butter
3 cups ground oatmeal (use
    regular oatmeal and
    grind it in the blender)

1 tsp. baking soda
1 tsp. salt
2½ cups all-purpose flour

Blend all the ingredients together. After the dough is stiff enough to handle, turn it out onto a lightly floured work surface and knead until elastic.

Divide the dough into 8 pieces of equal size and roll each into a ball. With a rolling pin, roll each bun into a thin pancake, as thin as possible. The dough is very elastic and will hold, so don't worry about tearing.

Each piece will now be about the size of a dinner plate.

Heat a skillet, melt a little butter in it and cook each bread over medium heat until brown spots appear. Turn over and cook the other side.

Each side should take about 4 minutes to cook.

Serve warm or cold.

SCONES

Serve this bread with butter and jam or marmalade at your afternoon tea—it is very English!

Yield: 2 round loaves. Can be frozen.

2 cups flour
2 tsps. baking powder
1 tsp. sugar

½ tsp. salt
¾ stick soft butter
½ cup milk

Preheat the oven to 400 degrees.

Blend the first 4 ingredients together. Add the butter in little pieces and the milk. Mix everything together until blended, then place on a lightly floured work surface and knead in a little more flour if the dough is sticky.

Divide the dough into 2 pieces of equal size and shape these into two round buns. Place on a lightly buttered baking sheet and with a knife cut a cross on top of each bun. Make some random holes with a fork.

Place in the oven and bake until lightly brown on top, about 20 minutes.

Cool slightly, then break the buns along the cuts into quarters.
Serve warm.

BACON BARLEY BREAD

If you find it impossible to obtain barley flour, you can substitute rye flour; it will work almost as well.

Serve this bread with lentil or pea soup.

Yield: 1 round bread. Do not freeze.

5 strips of bacon
2 cups barley flour
1 tsp. salt
2 cups milk

Preheat the oven to 475 degrees.

Fry the bacon until crisp and save the bacon fat. Crumble the bacon.

In a mixing bowl blend the flour with the salt, add the milk, all of the bacon fat except for 1 tablespoon, and the crumbled bacon.

With the tablespoon of leftover bacon fat, grease a 10" cake pan and pour the well-blended batter into it.

Bake in the oven for about 20 minutes or until a cake tester comes out clean and the top is light brown.

Let the bread cool slightly in the pan before you invert onto a platter. Serve warm.

GOUGÈRE

Lots of eggs go into this bread to make it big, beautiful and puffy. Serve with a glass of Burgundy wine.

Yield: 1 large bread ring. Do not freeze.

2 cups milk
1 stick butter
1 Tbs. salt
¼ tsp. freshly ground black
    pepper
Dash of freshly grated
    nutmeg

2 cups flour
8 eggs
1¼ cups finely cubed
    imported Swiss cheese

Preheat the oven to 375 degrees.

Scald the milk and remove any skin that forms on top. Add the stick of butter, cut into little pieces. Then add the salt, black pepper, and nutmeg and bring the whole thing to a boil.

    Immediately stir in the flour, lower the heat, and with a wooden

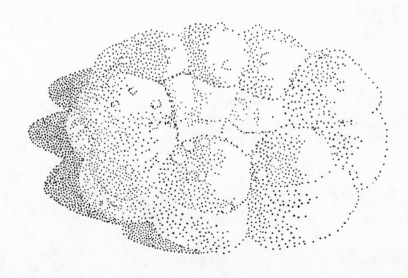

spoon stir the batter until it forms a ball and leaves the sides of the pot.

Transfer the stiff batter into a mixing bowl, add the eggs, 1 at a time, beating hard after each addition.

Add 1 cup of the cubed cheese to the batter.

Butter a baking sheet, and with 2 tablespoons scoop and shape pieces of dough into small ovals. Arrange the ovals in a circle on the baking sheet in 1 layer and then add another layer on top. Sprinkle the rest of the cubed cheese on top and bake in the oven for about 45 minutes or until the bread is golden and puffed. Make sure not to open the oven door for the first 30 minutes because the draft will make the bread fall.

Serve warm.

LAUFABRAUD
Leaf Bread

This is a very old bread, traditionally served at Christmas. It is unusual looking and also tastes very good.

Yield: 10 to 12 thin breads. Do not freeze.

1 cup milk
2 Tbs. butter
1 stick cinnamon
3 cups flour

½ tsp. salt
¼ tsp. baking powder
Shortening for frying (I prefer
  Crisco)

Bring to boil the milk with the butter and cinnamon stick.

Turn off the heat and let stand for 15 minutes.

Meanwhile mix together the flour, salt and baking powder; make a well in the center and add the milk mixture.

Stir until you have a stiff dough. Turn out onto a lightly floured work surface and knead for a couple of minutes. Then divide the dough into 10 pieces of equal size and place these on a floured baking sheet. Cover with a towel and let rest for 15 minutes.

Now with a rolling pin, roll each piece out as thin as possible. Don't worry, the dough will hold together.

Place a 7" to 8" plate on top of the dough and cut out rounds with a pastry wheel.

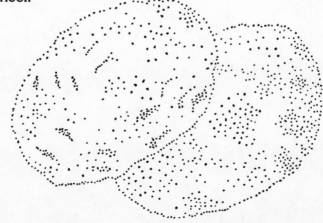

Place these rounds on wax paper, do not stack them, and let them stand uncovered to dry for about 20 to 30 minutes.

Now fold the dough double and, with a scissors, cut diagonal slits to form patterns in each thin round of dough (see illustrations). Use the same technique as when you cut out snowflakes or paper doilies.

Lift the little tips of each cut with a knife and fold backwards. Set aside. In a deep frying pan, melt some shortening, about ½" deep, and when hot fry 1 bread at a time for about 1 minute on each side.

Drain on several layers of paper toweling.

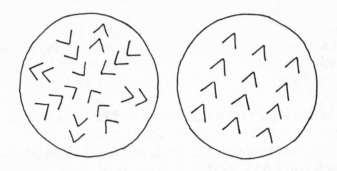

CHAPATI

These flat Indian breads are simple to make, and they're cooked on the top of the stove. They should be served freshly made and piping hot.

Yield: 8 to 10 chapati. Do not freeze.

2 cups whole-wheat flour   Warm water
½ cup all-purpose flour   ½ cup melted butter
1 tsp. salt

Blend the whole-wheat, all-purpose flour, and salt together in a bowl and add the warm water, a little at a time, blending until you have a rather stiff dough. Place the dough in a buttered bowl, cover and let it rest for about 1 hour.

Place the dough on your work surface (it should be lightly floured), pinch off pieces approximately the size of an egg, and roll out with a rolling pin until you have flat cakes with a 4″ to 5″ diameter.

Heat an ungreased skillet, preferably cast iron, and cook the chapati, about 4 or 5 at a time, until bubbles appear on top. Turn them and bake until they have light brown spots and are puffed up. Remove from the skillet, brush with the melted butter and wrap in a towel to keep them warm. Continue with the next batch of cakes until they are all done.

MRS. MENDIRATTAS'S LENTIL CHAPATI

These chapati can be served plain or with a filling. I prefer them with a very hot filling, served as hors d'oeuvres.

Yield: 16 filled turnovers. Can be frozen.

Chapati:
- 1½ cups whole-wheat flour
- ¼ cup light brown sugar
- 1 tsp. ground coriander
- 1 cup lentil puree (dhal)
- ½ cup water

Filling:
- 1 cup lentil puree (dhal)
- ¼ cup water
- ½ cup finely minced onions
- 1 tsp. salt
- 1 Tbs. very hot curry powder
- About ¼ cup vegetable oil for frying

Blend together the whole-wheat flour, brown sugar, salt, coriander and lentil puree. Stir in the water; then turn the dough out onto a lightly floured work surface. Knead for a couple of minutes, then put back in a bowl, cover with a towel and let rest for 1 hour.

Make the filling by blending all the ingredients in a bowl, to taste.

Turn the dough out and divide into 16 pieces of equal size; shape each piece into a ball and, with a rolling pin, roll out into thin cakes.

Place about 1 heaping teaspoon of filling on half the thin cake and fold the other half over. Then wet the edges with a little water to make the sides stick together.

Heat about ¼ cup vegetable oil in a skillet and fry the chapati, 3 or 4 at a time, for a couple of minutes on each side, or until light brown spots appear.

Drain on several layers of paper toweling and serve warm or cold.

CUMIN BALLS

Here is a real goodie, which my father brought back from a visit to India. I think they taste best warm with butter and honey and some very good tea, perhaps Darjeeling.

Yield: About 16 buns. Can be frozen.

1 egg	¼ tsp. salt
1 tsp. sugar	½ cup milk
1 stick very soft butter	2 cups flour
2 tsps. crushed cumin seeds	2½ tsps. baking powder

Preheat the oven to 425 degrees.

Beat the egg with the sugar and the butter until rather creamy. Add the cumin seeds and salt. Combine the flour and the baking powder and stir in, alternating with the milk. Start and end with the flour mixture.

Butter a baking sheet. Using 2 soup spoons, form balls about the size of an egg, and place on the baking sheet.

Bake for about 15 minutes or until light brown.

Serve warm.

WELL-BEHAVED BREAD

More like a thick pancake than anything else, this is one of the most delicious morsels you'll ever taste.

It is exotic and unforgettable. A hot wedge of this bread is a summer treat, when served outdoors with a cold drink.

If you simply can't get chick-pea flour, substitute all-purpose; it will be almost as good.

Yield: 1 bread. Do not freeze.

⅓ cup chick-pea flour
   (or all-purpose)
1 tsp. salt
½ cup thick yogurt
¼ tsp. ground hot chili
   pepper
3 Tbs. ground coriander

½ tsp. ground cloves
¼ tsp. ground cardamom
1 small, finely minced onion
3 egg yolks
2 Tbs. clarified butter
About 2 tsps. cumin seed to
   sprinkle on top

Place a small heavy frying pan or pot over medium heat. Pour the flour into the pan and stir constantly with a wooden spoon until the flour turns light brown.

Remove from the stove and pour into a mixing bowl.

Add the salt, yogurt, chili pepper, coriander, cloves and cardamom. Stir with a wooden spoon until everything is well blended and stiff.

Stir in the minced onions and the 3 egg yolks.

Heat the clarified butter in a small heavy frying pan, 8″ in diameter.

When the butter is hot pour in the batter to cover the bottom of the pan and cook over medium heat.

After a few minutes, check with a metal spatula to see if the underside has turned light brown. If so, carefully turn the bread over and continue to cook for a few minutes more, or until golden brown.

Transfer to a plate, sprinkle cumin seeds on top, cut into wedges and serve hot.

BANBRIDGE OATCAKES

A traditional Irish bread or cake that I like warm with butter and honey. These are crunchy and wonderful. Try to get really good, fresh oatmeal.

Yield: 12 small oatcakes. Do not freeze.

3 cups oatmeal   1 stick butter
½ tsp. salt   ⅓ cup water
½ tsp. baking soda

Preheat the oven to 350 degrees.

Place the oatmeal in the blender to grind.

Mix together 2 cups of the ground oatmeal with the salt and baking soda.

Melt the butter and add the water. Stir the butter-and-water mixture into the oat mixture and blend until you have a dough.

Sprinkle your work surface with the rest of the oatmeal and turn the dough onto it. Flatten the dough with your hands and, with the help of a rolling pin, roll out the dough until it is about ¼″ thick. Cut the dough into 12 squares of approximately the same size and place on an ungreased baking sheet.

Bake in the oven for about 20 minutes, then lower the heat to 300 degrees and toast the oatcakes until light brown.

Serve warm.

JACK AND DORIS SMITH'S IRISH SODA BREAD

Make this for St. Patrick's Day. It is so festive with the raisins and caraway seeds.

Yield: 2 round loaves. Can be frozen.

4 cups flour
1 tsp. salt
3 Tbs. baking powder
1 tsp. baking soda
1 Tbs. caraway seeds
1 cup raisins

½ stick butter
1⅔ cups sour milk (If you don't have sour milk squeeze the juice of 1 lemon into regular milk)

Preheat the oven to 375 degrees.

Sift together flour, salt, baking powder, and baking soda. Stir in caraway seeds and raisins. Add the butter, cut in little pieces, stir in the milk and blend until everything is mixed.

Place the dough on a lightly floured work surface and add some more flour if sticky. Knead a couple of times and divide into 2 equal pieces. Shape these into 2 large buns, flatten them a bit and place on a buttered cookie sheet.

With a knife cut a cross on top of each bun and bake in the oven for about 30 minutes or until puffed and pale golden.

Cool on a rack.

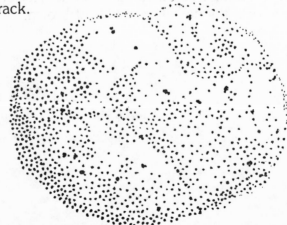

CORN BREAD

We like this version of Mexican corn bread, given to me by a Mexican friend. Served warm, it is nice and crumbly and goes well with a drink or even a glass of cold beer.

Such a pretty yellow, too!

Yield: 1 small loaf. Can be frozen.

1½ cups yellow cornmeal
½ cup all-purpose flour
3 tsps. baking powder
½ tsp. baking soda
1 tsp. salt
1 tsp. cayenne
2 eggs, slightly beaten

1 cup buttermilk
1 cup grated sharp cheese
1 cup cream-style corn
   (canned)
½ cup jalapeño peppers,
   chopped
½ cup corn oil

Preheat the oven to 375 degrees.

Sift together the cornmeal, flour, baking powder, baking soda, salt and cayenne. Add the 2 eggs, buttermilk, grated cheese, creamed corn, jalapeño peppers and oil, and stir until well blended.

Pour the batter into a well-oiled, small loaf pan (8" by 4") and bake for about 45 minutes or until a cake tester comes out clean.

Serve warm or cold.

POTATO LEFSE

A Norwegian friend once served us these thin flatbreads hot with butter and freshly chopped dill. They were sensational with cold beer.

You might also serve them with butter, sugar and cinnamon, but I prefer them with dill.

Yield: 12 flatbreads. Can be frozen.

2 cups cooked, mashed potatoes
1 tsp. salt
2 Tbs. melted butter

½ cup whole-wheat flour
½ cup all-purpose flour
¼ cup milk

Blend all the ingredients together until you have a smooth dough.

Place on a lightly floured work surface and knead, adding some more flour to make it manageable but still rather soft.

Divide the dough into 12 equal pieces and, with a rolling pin, roll each piece out as thin as you can without breaking. The dough is delicate and the *lefse* should be almost paper thin.

Place them on baking sheets sprinkled with flour. Heat a skillet on top of the stove, lower the flame to medium and cook 2 or 3 at a time in the skillet. (Do not use any shortening, they won't stick.)

Turn to cook the other side. They are ready when light brown spots appear.

Serve warm if possible.

BARRA MUFFINS

Ham and eggs and these muffins make a hearty breakfast. Put plenty of butter on the muffins and eat them warm.

Yield: 18 muffins. Can be frozen.

2 cups flour
2 tsps. baking powder
½ tsp. salt
¼ tsp. mace

2 eggs
½ stick butter
1 cup milk
½ cup grated sharp cheese

Preheat the oven to 400 degrees.

Sift together the flour, baking powder, salt and mace.

Make a well in the center and add the eggs and the butter, cut into little pieces. Stir to mix slightly.

Add the milk and cheese and stir. Do not overbeat the batter.

Spoon into buttered muffin tins and bake for about 20 minutes or until pale golden.

Serve hot.

OATCAKE

The Scots grow the most wonderful oat and here is one way of using that grain.

We like oatcake for breakfast with butter and blackberry jam.

Yield: 1 large flat bread. Can be frozen.

1 cup finely ground oatmeal   ½ tsp. baking soda
   (use regular oatmeal and   ½ tsp. salt
   grind it up in the   3 Tbs. melted butter
   blender)   1 tsp. honey
¼ cup all-purpose flour   4 Tbs. boiling water

Preheat the oven to 400 degrees.

Blend the dry ingredients together. Add the butter, honey and boiling water and stir until you have a well-blended dough.

Turn the dough out onto a work surface that has been sprikled with finely ground oatmeal, and knead until smooth.

With a rolling pin, roll the dough out until it is very thin and place on a buttered baking sheet. (I use a pizza pan for this purpose.)

Bake in the oven for 15 to 20 minutes or until the edges are light brown.

Serve warm or cold.

SURMJÖLKSBRÖD
Buttermilk Bread

A quick bread, redolent with spices. Do not cut or eat the bread until the next day, then serve with butter and cheese.

Yield: 1 round loaf. Can be frozen.

3 cups rye flour	1 tsp. crushed fennel seeds
2 cups all-purpose flour	1 tsp. anise seeds
2 tsps. baking soda	½ tsp. ground cumin
1 tsp. baking powder	⅓ cup dark corn syrup
½ tsp. salt	2 cups buttermilk

Preheat the oven to 325 degrees.

Sift together the flours, baking soda and baking powder.

Add the salt, fennel, anise and cumin. Stir in the syrup and milk, stirring until everything is well blended.

Pour the batter into a well-buttered 9″ cake pan and bake about 1 hour or until the top is browned and a cake tester comes out clean.

Take the bread out of the pan and let cool wrapped in a towel.

Serve the next day.

BOSTON BROWN BREAD

Boston brown bread is a must when you serve New England–style baked beans. It is cooked on top of the stove instead of in the oven, is easy to make and tastes great.

Yield: 2 small loaves. Can be frozen.

1 cup whole-wheat flour	½ cup molasses
1 cup rye flour	1¾ cups milk
1 cup cornmeal	Juice of 1 lemon
2 tsps. salt	1 cup raisins
1 tsp. baking soda	2 Tbs. all-purpose flour
2 tsps. water	

In a large mixing bowl blend together the 3 flours with the salt. In another bowl stir together the baking soda with the water and add the molasses. Squeeze the juice of the lemon into the milk, which will turn it sour. Mix the raisins with the 2 tablespoons of flour and stir all the ingredients into the flour mixture, stirring until everything is well blended and no lumps remain.

Butter two 1-pound coffee cans well and divide the batter into them. Cover the tops tightly with foil.

Place the 2 cans on a rack in a large kettle, and pour boiling water into the kettle until it reaches halfway up the coffee cans. Cover the kettle with a lid and let simmer for 3 hours, adding more water if some of it boils away.

After 3 hours, uncover the cans and check with a skewer to see if the breads are ready. If the skewer comes out clean, remove the cans immediately and turn the breads onto a platter to cool slightly.

Serve warm and cut with a string, never with a knife.

CORNSTICKS

You will need a cast-iron cornstick pan for these. We like them for breakfast with butter and marmalade.

Yield: 12 cornsticks. Can be frozen.

2 cups yellow cornmeal
1 Tbs. sugar
½ tsp. salt
2 tsps. baking powder

1 egg, slightly beaten
1 cup milk
2 Tbs. melted shortening

Preheat the oven to 450 degrees.

Blend the dry ingredients together; add the egg, milk and melted shortening and beat together.

Grease the cornstick pan and pour the batter into the forms.

Bake until golden, about 15 to 20 minutes. Remove the cornsticks and serve warm.

BREADS OF THE WORLD

CREAM CHEESE BISCUITS

The cheese makes these biscuits so light and flaky that they are almost like pastry.

Yield: 12 biscuits. Can be frozen.

1 cup flour
1 tsp. salt
1 stick butter
1 3 oz. package cream
    cheese

Preheat the oven to 425 degrees.

Sift together the flour and salt. Add the butter, piece by piece, and the cream cheese. Mix until you have a dough that holds together. Do not overmix.

Turn the dough out onto a lightly floured work surface and, with a rolling pin, roll it out to a thickness of about ½″. Cut out rounds with a biscuit cutter and place on a lightly buttered baking sheet.

Bake until pale brown, about 20 minutes. Serve warm with butter and jam.

NEW ENGLAND BRAN MUFFINS

A tasty, moist muffin that is particularly good for the elderly who need a diet rich in roughage. The molasses gives the muffins an appealing, sweet flavor.

Butter, jam or even cream cheese goes well with these.

Yield: 18 muffins. Can be frozen.

2 cups bran
1 cup whole-wheat flour
½ tsp. salt
1 tsp. baking soda
½ cup molasses

1½ cups milk
4 Tbs. melted shortening or
    vegetable oil (not olive
    oil)

Preheat the oven to 375 degrees.

Blend all the ingredients together and mix well.

Pour into buttered muffin tins and bake about 20 to 25 minutes or until lightly colored and a cake tester comes out clean.

Cool wrapped in a towel.

POPOVERS

These popovers are guaranteed to pop, and they are delicious too!

Yield: 12 popovers. Do not freeze.

3 eggs
1 tsp. sugar
1½ cups flour

¼ tsp. salt
1 cup milk
1 tsp. melted lard

Preheat the oven to 450 degrees.

Beat the eggs with the sugar until very thick and pale.

Combine the flour and salt with the milk, stirring until smooth; then stir in the lard. Add to the egg mixture and beat for a couple of minutes.

Pour into buttered muffin tins and bake in the oven for 20 minutes, then lower the temperature to 350 degrees and continue to bake for another 10 minutes.

Serve at once.

SOUTHERN SWEET POTATO BREAD

This sweet potato bread is almost like a pudding. It has an interesting spicy flavor and is almost too good to believe when served with chicken, preferably southern fried.

Yield: 1 bread. Do not freeze.

1 stick melted butter
2 cups mashed, cooked
    sweet potatoes
3 Tbs. light brown sugar
1 tsp. freshly grated nutmeg

1 tsp. ground allspice
Pinch of salt
⅓ cup flour
1 tsp. baking powder
2 eggs, slightly beaten

Preheat the oven to 425 degrees.

In a large bowl, with an electric mixer, blend the melted butter with the mashed sweet potatoes. Stir in the sugar and the ground spices and salt. Blend the baking powder with the flour and incorporate. Finally add the 2 eggs.

Pour into a square pan (9" by 9"). Bake in the oven for about 40 minutes or until lightly brown on top.

Serve warm or cold directly from the baking pan.

BREADS OF THE WORLD

SPOON BREAD

Place the entire spoon bread casserole on the center of the table, fresh from the oven, and eat it with butter.

It is so light, yellow and delicious that it will be gone in a couple of minutes.

Yield: 1 bread. Do not freeze.

2 cups water
1 cup yellow cornmeal
2 tsps. salt
½ stick of butter

1 cup milk
3 eggs, separated
1½ tsps. baking powder

Preheat the oven to 400 degrees.

Bring the water to a boil, stir in the cornmeal and salt and cook over medium heat until thick, stirring constantly.

Remove from the stove and add the butter to melt in the cornmeal mixture.

Stir in the milk and with an electric mixer beat until smooth. Beat in the 3 egg yolks, 1 at a time, beating hard after each addition. Beat in the baking powder.

Beat the egg whites until stiff and fold them into the cornmeal mixture.

Butter an 8″ casserole and pour in the batter.

Bake in the oven for about 35 minutes or until a cake tester comes out clean.

Serve at once.

10
SWEET QUICK BREADS

CITRUS BREAD

A friend from Barbados always serves this bread with tea. The bread has a lovely color and a true citrus flavor.

Yield: 1 small loaf. Can be frozen.

2 cups flour
3 tsps. baking powder
⅓ cup sugar
½ tsp. salt
Grated rind of 1 orange
Grated rind of 1 lemon (on the green side)

1 cup orange juice, freshly squeezed
1 egg, slightly beaten
½ stick melted and cooled butter

Preheat the oven to 375 degrees.

In a mixing bowl mix together the flour, baking powder, sugar and salt. Add the grated rind, orange juice, egg and melted butter.

Mix until well blended and pour into a small (8" by 4") buttered loaf pan.

Bake for about 40 minutes or until the top is golden and a cake tester comes out clean.

Cool slightly before removing from the pan, then continue to cool on a rack.

CORN BREAD

A rather crumbly bread with a tantalizing flavor. It tastes good served warm with butter and jam.

Yield: 2 small loaves. Can be frozen.

2 sticks soft butter
2 Tbs. sugar
3 eggs
2 cups yellow cornmeal
1½ cups all-purpose flour
3 Tbs. baking powder

1 tsp. ground ginger
½ tsp. salt
½ cup coconut milk
½ cup heavy cream
2 cups freshly grated coconut

Preheat the oven to 375 degrees.

Beat the butter with the sugar until light and fluffy. Beat in the eggs, 1 at a time.

In a separate bowl mix the cornmeal with the all-purpose flour, baking powder, ginger and salt. Add this to the butter mixture alternately with the coconut milk and the cream and stir until well blended. Stir in the grated coconut.

Pour into two small (8" by 4") loaf pans that have been buttered, and bake in the oven for about 35 to 40 minutes or until a cake tester comes out clean.

NOTE: You must use fresh coconut, never the canned or bagged kind. One coconut is more than enough for the above recipe.

The best tool to use for grating coconut is a coconut grater. It is a simple little device that looks somewhat like a small rake.

However, if you cannot buy one, you can use your blender with almost the same result. The main thing to remember is to use only *fresh* coconut.

PUMPKIN BREAD

You might use your leftover Halloween pumpkin for this spicy bread. Canned pumpkin or Mother Hubbard squash can also be used.

If you use fresh pumpkin or squash, cook it in a little water and puree in the blender.

Yield: 1 large bread. Can be frozen.

1¾ cups flour
1 tsp. baking powder
1 tsp. baking soda
½ tsp. salt
1 cup sugar
1 tsp. ground cloves
½ tsp. cinnamon
½ tsp. freshly grated nutmeg

2 eggs
½ cup vegetable oil (not olive oil)
2 cups pureed pumpkin
½ cup water
1 cup raisins
1 cup chopped dates

Preheat the oven to 350 degrees.

Measure the first 8 (dry) ingredients into a mixing bowl. Add the 2 eggs, oil, pumpkin and water. Stir until well blended. Stir in the raisins and chopped dates and pour into a large (9" by 5") loaf pan.

Bake in the oven for about 1½ hours or until a cake tester comes out clean.

If the top browns too quickly, cover with a piece of foil.

Let the bread cool in the baking pan for 5 minutes, then remove it and continue to cool wrapped in a towel.

Do not cut until the next day.

BREADS OF THE WORLD

CURRANT MUFFINS

Delicious when freshly made just in time for afternoon tea.

Yield: 12 muffins. Can be frozen.

2 cups flour
2 tsps. baking powder
3 Tbs. sugar
Pinch of salt
1 egg, beaten

1 cup milk
½ stick of butter, melted and
    cooled
1 cup currants

Preheat the oven to 425 degrees.

Blend together the flour, baking powder, sugar and salt. In a separate bowl blend the egg with the milk and the melted butter. Add to the dry ingredients, blending lightly so that you still have some lumps. Stir in the currants and pour the batter into buttered muffin pans. Bake for about 20 minutes or until golden.

LEMON BREAD

This is the perfect bread to serve with tea. It actually improves with age, but is excellent when served warm, too.

Yield: 1 bread. Can be frozen.

1 cup soft butter
⅔ cup sugar
4 eggs
2½ cups flour
2 tsps. baking powder

½ tsp. salt
1 cup milk
1 cup finely chopped walnuts
Grated rind of 1 lemon
Juice of 1 lemon

Preheat the oven to 350 degrees.

With an electric mixer beat together the butter and the sugar. Then blend in the eggs. Into this mixture incorporate the flour, baking powder and salt, alternately with the milk. Stir in the walnuts and grated lemon rind.

Pour the batter into a (9″ by 5″) loaf pan which has been buttered and dusted with flour.

Bake for about 1 hour, or until a cake tester comes out clean.

Remove from the oven, and with a skewer make random holes in the top; squeeze the lemon juice into them.

Cool on a rack.

HONEY BREAD

A very old recipe. This bread is usually served for breakfast or you might like to serve it with afternoon tea. It slices well and will keep for months in a bread box.

Yield: 1 large loaf. Can be frozen.

¾ cup honey
¾ cup light brown sugar
1½ cups rye flour
2 cups all-purpose flour
2 tsps. baking soda
1 tsp. ground ginger

1 tsp. cinnamon
1 tsp. allspice
Dash of salt
2 cups milk (can be sour)
3 Tbs. orange marmalade

Preheat the oven to 350 degrees.

Using an electric mixer beat the honey with the light brown sugar until it turns light. Sift together the two flours with the baking soda, ginger, cinnamon, allspice and salt. Mix into the honey-and-sugar, alternately adding the milk, but starting and ending with the dry ingredients.

Stir in the marmalade, mixing well.

Pour the batter into a large (9" by 5") loaf pan and bake in the oven for about 1¼ hours or until a cake tester comes out clean. If the top browns too quickly, cover with a piece of foil.

Cool wrapped in a towel and do not slice until the next day.

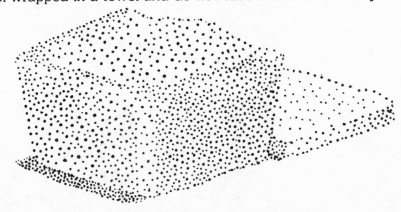

BREAKFAST OR TEA BREAD

This bread is so light and delicate that it might more aptly be called a cake.

Serve immediately after you remove from the oven, with your breakfast or with some fine tea.

Yield: 1 small loaf. Do not freeze.

4 egg whites
⅓ cup sugar
1 stick melted and cooled
    butter
¼ cup heavy cream

¼ tsp. saffron
¼ tsp. powdered cardamom
1 cup flour
½ tsp. baking powder

Preheat the oven to 350 degrees.

Beat the egg whites until white and fluffy. Beat in the sugar, a little at a time, and continue beating until the egg whites stand in soft peaks.

Blend the spices and the melted butter into the heavy cream.

Sift the flour with the baking powder. Carefully fold the flour mixture into the beaten egg whites, alternating with the cream-spice-and-butter mixture.

Butter a small (8″ by 4″) loaf pan and line it with wax paper, which you also butter.

Carefully pour in the batter and bake for about 40 to 45 minutes or until a cake tester comes out clean.

Serve at once.

POORI WITH A SWEET FILLING

These pastries have an exotic flavor. Looking at them gives no hint of what they are like inside, so that the filling comes as a real surprise.

Yield: 20 filled breads. Can be frozen.

Poori:

3 cups whole-wheat flour
⅓ cup vegetable oil (not olive oil)

About 1 cup water (enough to make a stiff dough)

Filling:

1 cup freshly grated coconut (not the canned or bagged sweetened kind)
¼ cup chopped raisins
Grated rind of ½ lemon

¼ tsp. ground cloves
½ tsp. ground cardamom
¼ cup coconut milk
About ¼ cup vegetable oil for frying

To make the *poori:* mix together the flour, vegetable oil and enough water to make a stiff dough. Cover with a towel and let stand in a warm place for 1 hour.

Meanwhile make the filling by mixing together all the ingredients and stirring until well blended.

Turn the dough out and knead for a couple of minutes. Divide into 20 pieces of equal size and roll into little balls.

With a rolling pin, roll each piece of dough until you have a very thin, round, pancakelike shape. Place about 1 tablespoon of filling on half the pancake and fold the other half over, wetting the edges with a little water to make the sides stick together.

Heat about ¼ cup vegetable oil in a skillet and fry each filled bread over medium heat for a few minutes on each side or until light brown spots appear.

Drain on several layers of paper toweling and serve warm or cold.

LIBERIAN RICE BREAD

Not as strong in flavor as the rice bread from Sierra Leone (see page 280), but this bread has a delicate, lovely banana flavor and a wonderful texture.

Yield: 1 large loaf. Can be frozen.

2 cups cream of rice (you'll find this among cereals in the supermarket)
4 tsps. baking powder
4 bananas (enough mashed bananas to make 2 cups)

½ tsp. salt
⅓ cup sugar
2 eggs, slightly beaten
1 cup milk
½ cup vegetable oil (not olive oil)

Preheat the oven to 350 degrees.

Mix the first 4 ingredients together in a mixing bowl. Mash the bananas, add the eggs, milk and vegetable oil and beat until smooth. Add the dry ingredients to this mixture and blend well.

Pour the batter into a large (9" by 5") well-buttered loaf pan and bake in the oven for about 1 hour or until a cake tester comes out clean.

Remove from the baking pan after a few minutes and cool wrapped in a towel.

SWEDEN

HASTBULLAR
Quick Buns

You can make such delicious buns just using baking powder!

Serve these warm either for breakfast or with afternoon coffee or tea.

Yield: 12 buns. Can be frozen.

1 stick soft butter
⅓ cup sugar
1 egg
½ cup milk
½ tsp. salt
½ tsp. crushed cardamom
    seeds

Grated rind of ½ lemon
2 cups flour
3 tsps. baking powder
½ cup raisins
1 beaten egg to brush the
    tops

Preheat the oven to 425 degrees.

In an electric mixer beat the butter with the sugar until pale. Add the egg, milk and salt, and stir in the cardamom and grated lemon rind.

Add the flour, mixed with the baking powder, and stir until you have a smooth batter that is rather stiff. Add the raisins and stir.

Butter muffin tins and spoon in the batter.

Brush with the beaten egg and bake in the oven for about 15 minutes or until golden. Serve warm or reheat wrapped in foil.

PEPPARKAKA
Spice Cake

In Sweden this is usually served with afternoon coffee, but I think it makes a much better tea bread. It keeps well and has a wonderful texture and flavor.

It may seem odd to use a coffee cup as a measure, but this is the way the recipe has been used for many, many years and it always comes out perfect. Just be sure that you use a medium-size coffee cup for all the ingredients.

Yield: 2 small loaves. Can be frozen.

4 eggs	3 tsps. baking soda
1 coffee cup of sugar	1 tsp. cinnamon
1 coffee cup of milk (sour is fine)	1 tsp. ground ginger
	2 tsps. ground cloves
1 coffee cup of heavy cream	5 Tbs. orange marmalade
1 stick butter, melted and cooled	2 Tbs. canned lingonberries or cranberries
4 coffee cups of flour	

Preheat the oven to 350 degrees.

Beat the eggs with the sugar and stir in the milk, heavy cream and melted butter.

Mix together the flour, baking soda, cinnamon, ginger and cloves and add to the liquid.

Stir in the orange marmalade and lingonberries or cranberries and blend until you have a well-mixed, soft batter.

Pour the batter into 2 small (8" by 4") loaf forms, or better still, 2 small fancy pans, either round or loaf shaped, that have been buttered and sprinkled with bread crumbs.

Bake in the oven for about 1 hour or until a cake tester comes out clean.

Leave in the pans for 5 minutes, then invert onto a plate and continue to cool wrapped in a towel. Do not slice until completely cool, preferably the next day.

SPICY ALMOND BREAD

This recipe was given to me by the wife of a Turkish diplomat and I like it very much with either tea or coffee.

Yield: 1 small loaf. Can be frozen.

2 eggs
⅔ cup honey
½ cup heavy cream
¾ cup melted butter
1 cup ground almonds

1 tsp. ground cloves
1 tsp. crushed anise seeds
2 cups flour
1 tsp. baking powder

Preheat the oven to 350 degrees.

Beat together the eggs and honey, add the cream and the melted butter. Stir in the ground almonds, cloves, anise seeds and the flour with the baking powder. Stir until well blended, then pour the batter into a small (8" by 4") buttered loaf pan and bake for about 1 hour or until a cake tester comes out clean.

Cool on a rack and do not slice until the next day; then slice very thinly.

BLUEBERRY MUFFINS

BREADS OF THE WORLD

Who wouldn't be happy to be served these for breakfast, still hot from the oven!
    Break in two and spread with lots of butter.

Yield: 12 muffins. Can be frozen.

2 cups flour	1 egg, slightly beaten
2 tsps. baking powder	1 cup milk
5 Tbs. sugar	½ stick melted butter
Pinch of salt	1 cup fresh blueberries

Preheat the oven to 425 degrees.

Blend together the flour, baking powder, sugar and salt.
    In a separate bowl blend the egg, milk, and melted butter. Add to the dry ingredients, blending lightly so that you still have some lumps.
    Stir in the blueberries and pour the batter into buttered muffin tins.
    Bake for about 20 minutes or until golden.
    Serve at once or reheat wrapped in foil.

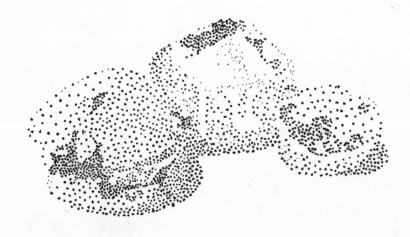

CORN MUFFINS WITH ORANGE

Eat them warm with butter for breakfast. The cornmeal and orange rind give wonderful flavor and texture to these muffins.

Yield: 18 muffins. Can be frozen.

1 cup yellow cornmeal
½ cup sugar
2 cups all-purpose flour
½ tsp. salt
1 tsp. baking soda
1 tsp. baking powder

Grated rind of 1 large orange
2 eggs, slightly beaten
1 stick melted and cooled
    butter
⅔ cup sour cream
⅓ cup milk

Preheat the oven to 375 degrees.

In a large mixing bowl blend together the 6 dry ingredients. Add the grated orange rind, the eggs, melted butter, sour cream and milk.

Stir until well blended.

Spoon into well-buttered muffin tins and bake for 20 to 25 minutes or until golden.

Serve at once or reheat wrapped in foil.

PHILPY

This specialty from Charleston should be served right away while hot.
We like it for breakfast, cut into wedges and spread with peach, apricot or strawberry jam.

Yield: 1 small bread. Do not freeze.

1¾ cups water
½ cup long-grain rice
¼ tsp. salt
2 Tbs. sugar

2 eggs, slightly beaten
½ cup rice flour (can be obtained in a health-food store)

Preheat the oven to 400 degrees.

Bring the water to a boil, stir in the rice and salt, lower the heat to low and cook until the rice is soft, about 35 to 40 minutes.

Mash the rice well; I have found that a potato ricer works best for this.

Place the rice in a mixing bowl and stir in the rice flour, the 2 eggs and the sugar. Stir until well blended. Then spoon the batter into an 8″ pie dish which has been well buttered.

Place in the oven and bake for about 20 minutes or until the top starts to turn a pale gold.

Cut into wedges and serve at once.

PECAN BREAD

Serve this bread the day after baking, spread with cream cheese or plain. Either way it is delicious.

Yield: 1 small loaf. Can be frozen.

2 cups flour
2 tsps. baking powder
½ tsp. baking soda
½ tsp. salt
½ tsp. cinnamon
Dash of freshly grated
nutmeg

¾ cup light brown sugar
1 heaping cup chopped
pecans
1 egg, slightly beaten
1 cup buttermilk
3 Tbs. melted butter

Preheat the oven to 350 degrees.

Sift together the flour, baking powder, baking soda, salt, cinnamon, and nutmeg. Add the brown sugar and chopped pecans. Stir in the egg, buttermilk and melted butter. Stir until smooth.

Pour the batter into a small (8" by 4") buttered loaf pan and bake for about 45 minutes or until a cake tester comes out clean.

Remove from the baking pan after 5 minutes and cool on a rack.

BREADS OF THE WORLD

RICE BREAD

This is especially popular in Sierra Leone, where it is served on every holiday. It is a rather heavy bread, so slice it thinly and enjoy.

Yield: 1 small loaf. Can be frozen.

1¾ cups rice flour (can be obtained in a health-food store)
2½ tsps. baking powder
½ tsp. baking soda
½ tsp. salt
½ cup sugar

½ to 1 tsp. freshly grated nutmeg
2 large bananas, mashed
¼ cup vegetable oil (not olive oil)
½ cup lukewarm water
½ cup dried currants

Preheat the oven to 325 degrees.

Sift together the first 6 ingredients in a mixing bowl.

With a potato masher mash the bananas and add the vegetable oil, water and currants.

Stir into the dry mixture and blend well.

Butter a small (8″ by 4″) loaf pan and pour in the rather stiff batter. Bake in the oven for about 1 hour or until a cake tester comes out clean.

Leave in the pan for a few minutes after it is done, then remove and continue to cool on a rack.

BEOGRADSKA PITA
Buns from Beograd

Small, fruit-filled and rather dry buns that go well with tea.

Yield: 15 small buns. Can be frozen.

3 eggs	Grated rind of 1 lemon
¾ cup sugar	2 cups flour
Dash of cinnamon	½ tsp. baking powder
1½ cups blanched and finely chopped almonds	¼ cup diced candied fruit

Preheat the oven to 375 degrees.

Beat the eggs with the sugar until pale and fluffy. Add the cinnamon and grated lemon rind and almonds.

Sift together the flour and baking powder and add that to your mixture. Stir in the diced candied fruit.

Place the dough on a floured work surface and knead, adding a little more flour if it is very sticky.

Divide the dough into 15 pieces of equal size and roll each piece into an oblong cylinder, about 2" long. Place on a buttered baking sheet.

Bake until lightly colored, about 25 minutes. Cool wrapped in a towel.

11
PANCAKES AND WAFFLES

Pancakes are eaten all over the world. A versatile dish, they can be eaten as hors d'oeuvres, accompaniments to soup, entrées or desserts. They lend themselves to a thrifty use of leftovers or to the addition of an elegant filling or sauce.

Since this basic recipe contains no sugar it can be used with both savory and sweet additions or fillings to make crepes, blintzes, palatschinken, *plättar* or almost any other kind of pancake.

These pancakes can be stacked with wax paper in between and frozen. They can then be thawed, filled and reheated when you need them.

It is not difficult to make them very thin, and they don't break easily.

Yield: 12 to 14 pancakes. Can be frozen.

Basic batter:
 5 eggs
 ½ tsp. salt

 1½ cups flour
 2 cups milk

Beat the eggs with an electric mixer. Add the salt, flour and milk, and beat until just mixed. Let stand for at least 30 minutes before cooking.

Heat a (10″ to 11″) cast-iron skillet over high heat, lower the heat slightly and melt a little butter in the pan. Pour about 1 soup ladleful of batter onto the skillet. Using a metal spatula spread the batter so that it covers the entire bottom of the skillet. Cook until the top is dry, then turn and cook the other side.

Serve immediately, filled or sauced. Or cool and reheat on flambé later. Or cool, stack and freeze.

BASIC MIX FOR PANCAKES AND WAFFLES, AMERICAN-STYLE (I)

This is a wonderful item to keep in the refrigerator, especially if you tape a label on top of the lid explaining what it is and how to use it.

This recipe makes a large quantity of mix that can be stored for later use so even your children can prepare their own quick meals.

Basic pancake mix:

11 cups unbleached flour
1 cup wheat germ

2 Tbs. salt
4 Tbs. baking powder

Measure all the ingredients into a large bowl and, with a big wooden spoon, stir until completely blended.

Pour into a large container for which you have a lid, such as a plastic or glass jar, and keep in the refrigerator.

Tape the following recipe on the lid:

Yield: Serves 4.

PANCAKES, WAFFLES:

2 cups basic pancake mix
1¼ cups milk
2 eggs, beaten

2 Tbs. melted butter or vegetable oil (not olive oil)

Stir everything together, mixing just until blended. The batter should still be lumpy.

Bake on a hot, greased griddle, or in a waffle iron.

For blueberry pancakes, add 1 cup of fresh blueberries before cooking.

PALATSCHINKEN

These are the dessert-loving Austrians' version of pancakes. Instead of jam you might serve them with sugared, halved strawberries and whipped cream.

Yield: 12 to 14 palatschinken,
or enough to serve 6. Once filled, do not freeze.

Use the basic recipe for thin
pancakes (see page 285)

plus:

1 cup strawberry or apricot
 jam
Confectioners' sugar

1 Tbs. cognac, brandy or
 other liqueur

Blend the jam with the cognac, brandy or liqueur and spread on each warm pancake. Roll the pancakes up into cylinders and place on a heated platter.

Sift confectioners' sugar on top and serve at once.

PFANNKUCHEN FUR SUPPE
Pancakes for Soup

Yield: Enough pancakes to
serve 6 to 8 people. Can be frozen.

Pancakes make a delightful and delicious addition to a clear soup. Use the basic recipe for thin pancakes (see page 285), and roll them up tightly after they are cooked.

Cut the rolled-up pancakes into pieces about ¼″ wide, place in large soup bowls and pour the hot, clear soup over them.

CREPES FLAMBÉ

Yield: 12 to 14 crepes,
or enough for 6 people. Do not freeze.

Use the basic recipe for thin pancakes (see page 285) and sprinkle each with sugar. Fold into quarters and sprinkle the tops with some additional sugar. Place on a heatproof platter under the broiler for a minute or two so that the sugar caramelizes.

Pour about ¼ cup cognac, rum or other liqueur over the pancakes and ignite.

Serve at once.

BREADS OF THE WORLD

THIN PANCAKES WITH MEAT, SEAFOOD OR VEGETABLE FILLING

Use the basic recipe for thin pancakes (see page 285) with a filling of either meat, seafood or vegetables.

Yield: About 12 to 14 filled pancakes, or enough for 6 people.

Do not freeze the filled pancakes.

Filling:
½ stick butter
4 Tbs. flour
1½ cups milk
½ tsp. salt
⅛ tsp. white pepper
Dash of freshly grated
nutmeg or ½ tsp.
paprika

2 cups of cooked meat,
seafood or vegetables
(cut into little pieces)

To make the filling: Melt the butter in a saucepan and stir in the flour, cooking for a couple of minutes while continuing to stir. Pour in the milk and continue to stir over low heat until thickened. Add the salt and spices and stir for another minute over low heat.

Stir in the cooked meat, seafood or vegetables. Fill the cooked pancakes and roll up into cylinders.

Serve at once while hot.

BLINIS

These are tiny yeast pancakes that are usually served with melted butter, sour cream and caviar. In Sweden they are served with the native caviar, *löjrom*, which is considered a great delicacy, and washed down with spicy aquavit.

The Russians, naturally, like their own caviar and vodka, and in Finland grated cheese and melted butter often top the blinis.

Thinly sliced smoked salmon, sturgeon, or tender herring fillets with dill and onions also make fine accompaniments.

Yield: 24 blinis. Do not freeze.

1 envelope yeast	1 cup buckwheat flour
¼ cup lukewarm water	¼ cup all-purpose flour
1 Tbs. light brown sugar	½ tsp. salt
1 cup milk	2 eggs, slightly beaten
2 Tbs. butter	2 stiffly beaten egg whites

Proof the yeast in the lukewarm water with the sugar.

Heat the milk and butter until the butter melts, let stand until lukewarm, then add to the yeast sponge.

Stir in the flour, salt and eggs, and mix well.

Cover the bowl with a towel and let stand in a warm place for 1½ hours.

Fold in the stiffly beaten egg whites.

Heat a cast-iron skillet over medium heat. Or, if you have one, use a Swedish *plättpanna*. Melt a little butter in the pan and spoon in the batter to make tiny pancakes. About 1 tablespoon for each blini is enough. When the bottom is lightly colored, turn and bake the other side.

Keep hot until ready to serve.

BREADS OF THE WORLD

CREPES SUZETTE

Do not flambé these crepes, but heat quickly over high heat and serve. Use the basic recipe for thin pancakes (see page 285).

Yield: About 12 to 14 crepes or enough for 6 people.
Do not freeze after the crepes are filled.

Filling:
    1 stick soft butter
    1½ cups confectioners' sugar
    Grated rind of 1 orange

    ¼ cup Grand Marnier or Curaçao

With an electric mixer beat together the ingredients for the filling until you have a smooth butter cream.

Spread one side of each cooked crepe, fold into quarters and place on a heatproof platter.

Just before serving, heat quickly over high heat or in a 450-degree oven. Sprinkle some sugar and additional Grand Marnier or Curaçao over the crepes and serve right from your cooking dish.

SCRIPELLE

Serve these savory pancakes with clear chicken broth. Place 2 in the bottom of a large soup plate and pour hot broth over them.

Good and nourishing on a chilly day.

Yield: About 12 to 14 pancakes. Can be frozen.

5 eggs
½ tsp. salt
1½ cups flour
2 cups milk
2 Tbs. minced parsley
Dash of freshly grated
    nutmeg

About 1 cup of freshly grated
    Parmesan cheese
A piece of salt pork to rub
    the skillet

Beat the eggs with an electric mixer. Add the salt, flour and milk, and beat until just mixed. Add the minced parsley and dash of nutmeg and let the batter stand for 1 hour.

Heat a (10" to 11") cast-iron skillet until very hot. Lower the heat a little and rub the cooking surface of the skillet with the piece of salt pork.

Pour about 1 soup ladle of batter onto the skillet and spread it out with a metal spatula. Cook for a couple of minutes on each side or until golden.

Sprinkle about 1 tablespoon of Parmesan cheese on the pancake after you remove it from the skillet, then roll up and keep warm until serving time.

BLINTZES

As a child I had an aunt in whose home blintzes were almost a meal in themselves.

Preceded by a not too rich soup, the blintzes were served with some sour cream and a little homemade cherry preserve. To drink, we enjoyed a glass of tea with a spoon of cherry preserve stirred into it.

Blueberry preserve is also very good or perhaps strawberry, raspberry or blackberry. Experiment to see what you like.

Use the basic recipe for thin pancakes (see page 285).

Yield: 12 to 14 blintzes or
enough for 6 people. Can be frozen.

Filling:
1 pound farmer cheese   1 Tbs. sugar
2 egg yolks   1 Tbs. sour cream
½ tsp. salt

Topping:
Sour cream
Fruit preserve

Blend the ingredients for the filling together and stir.

Place a couple of tablespoons of the cheese filling on each pancake and roll up. Tuck the ends in first so that the cheese is completely enclosed and the whole thing resembles a hot dog. Place on a platter and refrigerate.

Before serving, heat a little butter in a skillet and cook the blintzes until light brown and heated through.

Serve hot with sour cream and fruit preserve.

GRÄDDUÅFFLOR
Cream Waffles

The crispiest, most delicious and most fattening waffles you can imagine! Serve with whipped cream, strawberries and coffee.

These waffles are traditionally served on "Waffle Sunday," a day in late winter when you eat waffles for breakfast, lunch and dinner, and consequently get quite sick of waffles for the rest of the year.

Yield: Serves 4 people. Do not freeze.

Batter:
    2 cups heavy cream   1 tsp. sugar
    ½ cup club soda   Pinch of salt
    1½ cups flour

Topping:
    Whipped cream
    Strawberries

In an electric mixer whip the cream until thick but not stiff. Stir in the club soda, flour, sugar and salt until you have a smooth batter. Let the batter stand at room temperature for 1 hour.

Heat a waffle iron and butter lightly. Stir the batter before you cook the waffles. Pour a little batter onto the griddle and cook until light brown. Serve the waffles warm.

Do not stack the waffles on top of each other on the serving platter since that will make them go limp.

MOROTSPANNKAKOR
Carrot Pancakes

Where I come from, on the east coast of Sweden by the Baltic, when children refused to eat what was good for them their mothers always knew what to serve: carrot pancakes with whipped butter and chopped chives.

Children adore this delicious dish. The pancakes are a pretty yellow and with the chives they make for a colorful lunch.

Grown-ups love these too, perhaps with a squirt of lemon juice on top.

Yield: 6 pancakes. Do not freeze.

2 eggs
1 cup milk
¾ cup flour

2 large carrots, finely grated
Pinch of salt

Beat the eggs with the milk, add the flour, grated carrots and salt, and stir until well blended. Let stand for at least 20 minutes before you cook them.

Heat a (10" to 11") cast-iron skillet and melt a little butter in it. Turn the heat to medium and spoon out some batter, about a soup ladleful. Spread the batter with a metal spatula until it is about ¼" thick and cook.

When little bubbles appear on top, flip the pancake over and cook the other side until golden.

Serve hot with about ½ stick of soft butter that has been whipped with a couple of tablespoons of freshly chopped chives.

PLÄTTAR

Yield: About 30 *plättar*, or enough for 5 to 6 people.

Use the basic recipe for thin pancakes (see page 285) and bake in a Swedish *plätt* pan, if you have one. If not, bake in a regular skillet, but make the pancakes smaller, about 2½″ to 3″ in diameter.

Serve at once with whipped cream and lingonberry preserves or sugared with mashed strawberries or raspberries.

COCONUT PANCAKES

My father was an enthusiastic amateur cook, and since he spent a lot of time in the Far East, he naturally brought back many interesting recipes.

As a child these pancakes were my favorites, and when we were good they were our breakfast treat.

Yield: Enough for 6 people. Do not freeze.

4 eggs
1 cup fresh coconut milk, strained
½ tsp. salt
2 cups rice flour (can be bought in a health-food store or specialty shop)

¼ cup all-purpose flour
½ cup freshly grated coconut (not the canned or bagged, sweetened kind)

Beat the eggs until completely blended. Stir in the coconut milk, salt, rice flour and all-purpose flour. Stir until smooth and let stand for ½ hour.

Heat a (10″ to 11″) cast-iron skillet and melt a little butter in it. Reduce the heat to medium and pour in a little batter, about a soup ladleful, spreading thinly with a metal spatula. Cook until the bottom is golden, then turn over and cook the other side.

Fold into quarters, sprinkle with coconut and serve.

PANCAKES OR WAFFLES AMERICAN-STYLE (II)

Nothing can quite compare with these for breakfast on a cold or otherwise miserable morning.

You must serve them with butter, pure maple syrup and tiny pork sausages (maybe your own, homemade).

This is definitely the breakfast to serve visitors from overseas.

Yield: 18 small pancakes. Do not freeze.

2 cups flour
2 tsps. baking powder
½ tsp. salt
2 eggs, slightly beaten
3 Tbs. melted butter or
    vegetable oil (not olive
    oil)

1½ cups milk (if you use
    buttermilk, which you
    may, use a little more)

Stir the dry ingredients together, add the eggs, melted butter and milk, and blend quickly. Let stand for ½ hour.

Heat a skillet over medium heat, melt a little butter in it and drop spoonfuls of the batter onto the skillet. Turn the pancakes when small bubbles appear on top and continue to cook until both sides are lightly browned. Serve at once with butter and pure maple syrup. Along with sausages, try ham or bacon.

Use the same batter for waffles.

12
SANDWICHES

DANISH BEEF TARTARE SANDWICH

The ingredients for this sandwich have to be absolutely top grade. Do not use ground beef but buy a piece of beef fillet and with a sharp knife scrape the meat into tiny pieces.

Yield: 1 sandwich. Do not freeze.

1 slice of rye bread
1 pat of soft butter
About ⅓ cup freshly scraped
    fillet of beef
1 raw egg yolk

1 tsp. minced onion
1 tsp. capers
½ tsp. grated white
    horseradish

Lightly butter the slice of rye bread and spread the scraped meat on it, making sure to cover the bread completely and evenly.

Place the egg yolk on top of the meat on one-half the sandwich. Then place the minced onion, capers and horseradish in little heaps on the other half.

Serve at once with a glass of beer.

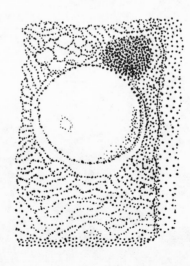

SHRIMP SANDWICH

This beautiful and delicious sandwich should be accompanied by a glass of Danish beer, if possible.

Yield: 1 sandwich. Do not freeze.

1 large slice of homemade white bread, lightly toasted
1 Tbs. mayonnaise mixed with ½ tsp. white horseradish

About ½ cup of tiny canned shrimp (comes in a glass jar or tin, usually from Greenland or Iceland)
Chopped fresh dill

Allow the toast to cool, then spread with the mayonnaise and horseradish mixture. Arrange the shrimps on top in a tempting heap and sprinkle with the chopped dill.

Eat with beer as a snack or for lunch.

CROÛTE SUISSE

A plain, good grilled cheese sandwich from Marseilles.
    You must use high-quality, pure olive oil, which is what gives this sandwich its distinct and appealing flavor.

Yield: 1 sandwich. Do not freeze.

1 thick, large slice French
    white bread, with the
    crust removed

A couple of Tbs. fine olive oil
2 slices Emmenthaler or
    Gruyère cheese

Sauté both sides of the bread in the olive oil. Then remove to a baking sheet and place the 2 slices of cheese on top.
    Place under the broiler until the cheese melts.
    Serve at once.

BREADS OF THE WORLD

CROQUE-MONSIEUR
Sandwich for a Man

This makes a nice lunch with a salad and a glass of wine.

Yield: 1 sandwich. Do not freeze.

2 slices of white bread,
    crusts removed
1 pat of soft butter
1 slice cooked ham
2 slices of Swiss cheese

Preheat the oven to 425 degrees.

Butter the 2 slices of bread. On 1 slice, layer a slice of cheese, the ham and the other slice of cheese.

Then place the other piece of bread on top, buttered side toward the cheese.

Place on a lightly buttered baking sheet and bake for 3 to 4 minutes or until the cheese begins to melt.

Another way of cooking the sandwich is to fry it in a buttered frying pan on both sides.

Serve at once.

CROQUE-MADAME
Sandwich for a Lady

Almost the same thing as the *croque-monsieur*, but substitute thinly sliced cooked chicken for the ham.

MUSSEL SANDWICH FROM PROVENCE

A rather unusual but really wonderful sandwich. You might serve it as an hors d'oeuvre or as part of a light lunch.

Yield: 4 sandwiches. Do not freeze.

4 slices of French bread, ½"
   thick
2 cups freshly cooked
   mussels or mussels
   canned in water

¾ stick soft butter
5 crushed garlic cloves
½ cup minced parsley
Dash of salt and pepper

Preheat the oven to 450 degrees.

Drain the mussels. Cream the butter and add the crushed garlic, parsley, salt and pepper. Divide the mussels between the four slices of bread and dot the butter-cream on top of the mussels.

Place on a lightly buttered baking sheet and bake in the oven for about 5 minutes.

Serve at once.

BREADS OF THE WORLD

CHECKERBOARDS

A nifty-looking sandwich which makes a perfect accompaniment to a spicy Bloody Mary.

Yield: 6 to 8 slices of pumpernickel sandwiches. Do not freeze.

6 to 8 slices very dark homemade pumpernickel, about ¼″ thick

About 8 ounces cream cheese.

Spread each slice of bread thickly and evenly with the cream cheese. Assemble the slices on top of each other. Chill in the refrigerator for about 1 hour.

Now take the sandwich out and slice it into 6 parts if you used 6 slices of bread, or 8 slices if you used 8.

You will now have zebra-striped sandwiches.

Now assemble these on top of each other so that you have a cube. Chill for another hour.

Take out and carefully slice into 6 or 8 slices, which will now look like checkerboards.

If the checkerboards are too big, quarter them for more bite-size morsels.

GUASTIEDDI
Cheese in a Bun

This is for a single serving, but after you have tasted one you may want more, so just increase the recipe accordingly.

Yield: 1 sandwich. Do not freeze.

1 crusty bun
2 Tbs. olive oil
1 thick slice ricotta cheese
(or if it is very soft, 2–3 Tbs.)

1 thick slice provolone cheese
¼ tsp. dry oregano

Preheat the oven to 400 degrees.

Split the roll and brush the cut sides with the olive oil. Place the ricotta and the provolone cheese on the bottom half. Sprinkle with oregano and, if you wish, some salt and freshly ground pepper. Replace the top, place on a lightly oiled baking sheet and bake for 5 to 10 minutes.
   Serve at once.

BREADS OF THE WORLD

MOZZARELLA IN CARROZZA
Fried Cheese Sandwich

In English this means "mozzarella in a wagon" which is a Neapolitan specialty.

Yield: 1 sandwich. Do not freeze.

2 slices Italian bread, crust
   removed
1 thick slice mozzarella
   cheese
1 garlic clove, crushed

¼ cup milk
2 Tbs. flour
1 well-beaten egg
2 Tbs. olive oil

Place the cheese and the crushed garlic between the 2 bread slices and press the sandwich down with the palm of your hand. Dip into the milk, the flour, and finally the well-beaten egg.

Fry in olive oil over medium heat until golden brown.

Serve at once.

APPELKALLE
Apple Sandwich

Here's something the children will adore.

Yield: 4 sandwiches. Do not freeze.

4 slices of day-old white
    bread, crust removed
2 Tbs. soft butter
2 tart apples

Dash of cinnamon
About ½ cup marzipan (the
    Danish kind)

Preheat the oven to 425 degrees.

Lightly butter a baking sheet and place the 4 bread slices on it. Butter the slices. Grate the apples, peel and all, on the coarse side of a grater and spread on top of the bread. Sprinkle some cinnamon on top.

    Grate the marzipan (also on the coarse side of the grater) and put on top of the grated apples.

    Place in the oven and bake until the marzipan turns a light gold. Serve warm.

CAVIAR SANDWICH

A truly luxurious sandwich that ought to be served with iced vodka or aquavit.

Yield: 1 sandwich. Do not freeze.

1 slice white bread, lightly
   toasted
1 pat soft butter
1 raw egg yolk

2 tsps. finely minced onion
3 Tbs. caviar
1 wedge lemon

Lightly butter the bread and place the raw egg yolk in the middle. Surround the yolk with the minced onion and surround that with the caviar. Place a lemon wedge on the side and serve at once.

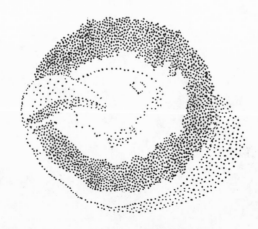

GRILLED SALAMI SANDWICH

A rather unusual grilled sandwich, excellent with a glass of beer.

Yield: 1 sandwich. Do not freeze.

1 slice homemade white bread	4 slices salami
1 pat soft butter	1 large tomato slice
About ½ tsp. mustard	1 thick slice Swiss cheese

Preheat the oven to 450 degrees.

Spread the butter on the bread and then a little mustard on top. Arrange the salami slices so that they cover the sandwich completely. Add the tomato slice and top with the slice of Swiss cheese.

Place on a lightly buttered baking sheet and bake until the cheese starts to melt.

Serve at once.

BREADS OF THE WORLD

GRILLED SWISS CHEESE SANDWICH

A little different from the American grilled cheese sandwich.
Nice for lunch or a midnight snack.

Yield: 1 sandwich. Do not freeze.

2 slices ¼"-thick white bread
2 thick slices imported Swiss
   cheese, the same size as
   the bread

2 slices of onion
½ tsp. hot paprika
Pat of butter

Preheat a griddle or if you don't have one, a cast-iron frying pan or skillet. Melt the butter and lower the heat to medium.

Take 1 slice of bread, place the 2 slices of onion on top, add the slices of Swiss cheese, sprinkle with paprika and place the other slice of bread on top.

In a griddle or frying pan, fry each side until golden and the cheese begins to melt.

Serve at once with a dill pickle.

ÖLSMORGAS

A hearty sandwich with a good strong taste, *Ölsmorgas* means a sandwich to eat with a glass of beer.

Yield: 1 sandwich. Do not freeze.

1 slice pumpernickel   ⅓ cup sliced mushrooms
1 medium-size onion,   Dash of salt and pepper
   chopped   1 Tbs. minced parsley

Sauté the chopped onion in a little butter. When it wilts add the sliced mushrooms and cook until they are light brown and a little crisp at the edges. Season and spread onto the slice of pumpernickel; sprinkle with minced parsley.
   Serve at once.

13
WHAT TO DO WITH LEFTOVER BREAD

HONEY CAKE

A truly delectable cake that you can make with leftover white bread. It stays fresh for at least a week if kept in the refrigerator.

Serve with whipped cream or mock Devonshire cream (see recipe below).

Yield: 1 rather thin cake. Do not freeze.

1 pound white bread (not fresh)	¾ cup honey
1½ sticks melted butter	1 cup ground almonds
	½ tsp. almond extract

Remove the crust from the bread and, using a blender, make bread crumbs of the bread.

Mix the melted butter with the bread crumbs, stir in the honey and ground almonds and, over medium heat, stir the mixture with a wooden spoon until it is well blended and has turned into a paste.

Turn off the heat and stir in the almond extract.

Line a 9″ spring form with wax paper and spoon the paste into the form, using your hands to pat it down. Cover and, after it has cooled, place in the refrigerator to chill.

Before serving remove from the spring form, peel off the wax paper and place on a serving platter.

MOCK DEVONSHIRE CREAM

With an electric mixer beat 3 ounces cream cheese with ½ cup heavy cream until thick and smooth. Use as a topping for the honey cake.

MOHR IM HEMD
Moor in a Shirt

The fanciest dish that you can make with leftover bread, this pudding is certainly not economical, but it is fun, looks festive and tastes extravagant.

Yield: 1 pudding. Do not freeze.

Several slices of stale, white
    bread (enough to make
    3 cups when broken into
    pieces)
¾ cup heavy cream
1 stick soft butter
¾ cup confectioners' sugar
5 eggs

2 egg yolks
2 Tbs. dark rum
1 cup ground walnuts
1 bar imported bittersweet
    chocolate, melted (3 oz.)
1 cup heavy cream,
    whipped, for decorating

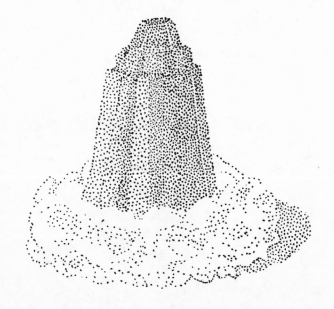

Soak the broken bread pieces in the heavy cream and set aside.

Beat the butter with the confectioners' sugar until creamy and pale. Add the eggs and the yolks, 1 at a time, beating well after each addition. Add the bread and the cream, and stir in the rum, ground walnuts and melted chocolate.

Stir until well blended.

Butter well a tall form of small diameter and pour in the batter. Cover the top of the mold with a lid or a piece of foil and put into a large saucepan which you have filled with boiling water almost to the top.

Cook over low heat until a cake tester comes out clean, which will take about 1½ to 2 hours.

Add more boiling water if necessary while you are cooking the pudding, as some of it may boil away.

Let the pudding cool for a couple of minutes, then unmold onto a platter and pipe the whipped cream around the base of the pudding. You now have a moor in a shirt!

Eat warm.

MUTTI' SEMMEL KNODELN
Bread Dumplings

Here is another ingenious way of using up stale bread.

Serve the dumplings with a clear soup and let your guests try to guess what they are made from.

Yield: 18 to 20 dumplings. Do not freeze.

3 cups bread cubes, cut
   from slightly stale white
   bread or rolls
½ stick butter
2 eggs, slightly beaten

1½ cups flour
½ tsp. baking powder
1 tsp. salt
Dash of white pepper
⅓ cup milk

Sauté the bread cubes in the butter until crisp but not browned.

Put the eggs, the flour, baking powder, salt and white pepper in a mixing bowl. Stir in the milk and blend until you have a smooth batter that is not too runny.

Stir in the bread cubes and let stand for ½ hour.

Meanwhile boil some lightly salted water in a large saucepan.

When the water is boiling hard drop the dough in with a tablespoon, about 5 or 6 tablespoons at a time.

Simmer the dumplings for 10 minutes, then remove with a slotted spoon and drain on several layers of paper toweling.

After you have finished cooking all the dumplings, place them on a buttered baking sheet and place in a 400-degree oven for about 7 minutes or until they turn light brown.

Serve at once in hot soup.

BREAD PUDDING

An elegant bread pudding, and the best one I have ever tasted.

Yield: Serves 6. Do not freeze.

½ cup raisins
¼ cup brandy
8 slices of stale French
    bread, crusts removed
2 Tbs. soft butter

2 cups milk
⅓ cup sugar
3 eggs
4 egg yolks
1 tsp. vanilla

Preheat the oven to 325 degrees.

Put the raisins in a bowl, pour the brandy over them and let soak for ½ hour.

Arrange the 8 slices of bread, which you have buttered on both sides, in a buttered baking dish.

Bring the milk to a boil, remove from the heat and stir in the sugar until completely dissolved.

With an electric mixer beat the eggs and the egg yolks; pour in the milk gradually and add the vanilla.

In the baking dish pour the raisins-and-brandy over the bread slices and then pour the egg mixture on top.

Put the baking dish in a pan of boiling water and bake in the oven for about 40 minutes or until a table knife inserted into the pudding comes out clean.

Let cool a little before serving, but serve while still warm. It is also good cold the next day.

PICATOSTES

What a lovely way to use up stale bread!
Serve these little goodies with some very strong hot chocolate.

Yield: Serves 4. Do not freeze.

About 3 cups of ¾"-thick
    bread cubes, cut from
    stale, white bread
1 to 2 cups milk (enough to
    soak the bread
    completely)

Pinch of salt
½ cup flour
Olive oil
Confectioners' sugar
Cinnamon (optional)

Soak the bread cubes in the milk mixed with the salt.
    Drain on several layers of paper toweling.
    Heat the olive oil in a large skillet. Dip the bread cubes in the flour and fry until golden, over medium heat.
    Pile the fried bread cubes high on a platter and sprinkle liberally with sifted confectioners' sugar and, if you like, a sprinkle of cinnamon.

SPANISH TOAST

Serve this dish as a dessert.

Yield: Serves 6. Do not freeze.

18 to 20 slices stale white
  bread
½ cup milk
4 eggs, well beaten
¼ cup sugar
¼ tsp. ground mace

Grated rind of 1 lemon
½ stick butter
¼ cup cream sherry
½ cup confectioners' sugar
½ cup toasted slivered
  almonds

Combine the milk with the beaten eggs, beating with a fork until well blended. Blend in the sugar, mace and grated lemon rind.

Melt some of the butter in a large skillet. Dip the bread slices in the egg mixture, a few at a time, then fry until golden. Transfer them to a hot platter.

After all the bread slices are fried, brush with the sherry and sprinkle the confectioners' sugar and almonds on top.

Serve immediately.

FATTIGMANS MIDDAG
Poor Man's Dinner

This makes a nice lunch with a green salad and some cold beer.

Yield: Serves 2. Do not freeze.

4 to 5 slices stale bread,
   white or rye
2 Tbs. soft butter
2 medium-size cold, boiled
   potatoes

1 medium-size onion
1 small tin of Scandinavian
   anchovy sprats
⅓ cup grated sharp cheese

Preheat the oven to 400 degrees.

Butter a small ovenproof dish.

Remove the crusts from the bread, butter the slices with the rest of the butter and place in the bottom of the baking dish.

Slice the potatoes thinly and place on top of the bread. Then chop the onion and sprinkle over the potatoes. Top with the anchovy sprats and sprinkle with the grated cheese.

Bake in the oven for about 7 minutes or until the cheese has melted and turned golden.

Serve at once.

SWISS APPLE AND BREAD DESSERT

A simple and good dessert that you might serve with some whipped cream or vanilla sauce.

Yield: Serves 4. Do not freeze.

½ stick butter
6 slices stale white bread,
   crust removed
3 green apples, peeled,
   cored and thinly sliced

½ cup sugar
½ tsp. cinnamon
½ cup raisins

Melt the butter in a rather large skillet. Cut the stale bread into small pieces and brown them in the butter.

Add the apple slices, cover and simmer until the apples are soft, about 10 to 15 minutes.

Stir in the sugar, cinnamon and raisins.

Serve warm with whipped cream or vanilla sauce.

WHAT TO DO WITH LEFTOVER BREAD

GARLIC-PARMESAN BREAD

Delicious with pasta and your favorite sauce.

Yield: 1 loaf.

1 loaf stale French or Italian
    bread
1 stick melted butter

6 cloves crushed garlic
½ cup freshly grated
    Parmesan cheese

Slice the bread into ¾"-thick slices.

Put the melted butter into a dish with the crushed garlic cloves.

Dip each slice of the bread into the garlic-butter mixture, then coat with the Parmesan cheese. Place the bread slices on a broiling pan and broil on both sides until they are golden brown. Serve hot.

ITALIAN-STYLE BREAD CRUMBS

Yield: 1 cup bread crumbs

1 cup bread crumbs (made
   from stale bread in a
   blender)
4 Tbs. freshly grated
   Parmesan cheese

3 Tbs. fresh, chopped
   parsley
2 tsp. dried oregano
½ tsp. salt
Dash of black pepper

Combine all the ingredients. Put in a glass jar with a twist-off lid.
   Keep in the refrigerator or freeze.

COUNTRY-BY-COUNTRY-INDEX

Arabic
Honeycake, 319
Mock Devonshire Cream, 319

Armenia
Peda Bread, 37

Austria
Kartoffelbrot, 38
Kaisersemmeln, 103
Faschingskrapfen, 141
Omilla's Buchteln, 143
Sour Cream Dough, 145
Striezel, 147
Topfen Kuchen, 149
Viennese Kugelhupf, 150
Zwetschkenkuchen, 152
Palatschinken, 287
Pfannkuchen fur Suppe, 288
Mohr im Hemd, 320
Mutti' Semmel Knodeln, 322

Barbados
Citrus Bread, 263

Belgium
Verviers Bread, 154

Brazil
Paezinhos De Cerveja, 105
Fruit Bread, 156

Canada
New Brunswick Oatmeal Bread, 39
Canadian Raisin Bread, 158
Bannock, 233

Caribbean
Corn Bread, 264
Pumpkin Bread, 265

Chile
Marylo Velasco's Empanadas Chilenas, 234

China
Hua Chuan (Rolls), 41

Cuba
Pan De Cuba De Afuera Dura, 42

Czechoslovakia
Karlsbad Buns, 106
Omilla's Buchteln, 143
Mährischer Kuchen, 159

Denmark
Kartoffelbrød, 44
Sour Bread, 45
Fladbrød, 236
Danish Beef Tartare Sandwich, 303
Shrimp Sandwich, 304

Egypt
Barley Bread, 47
Wheat Bread, 48

England
Graham Squares, 50
Cheese Baps, 108
Chelsea Buns, 160
Hot Cross Buns, 162
Pope Ladies, 164
Scones, 237
Currant Muffins, 266
Lemon Bread, 267

Ethiopia
Honey Bread, 52

Finland
Buckwheat Bread, 53
Finnish Rye Bread, 54
Pulla, 165
Bacon Barley Bread, 238
Blinis, 291

France
French Bread, 55
French Country Rye Bread, 57
Gannat Bread, 59
Walnut Bread from Burgundy, 60
Croissants, 109

332

Baba au Rhum, 167
Chocolate Buns, 169
Sourdough French Bread, 222
Gougère, 239
Crepes Flambé, 289
Crepes Suzette, 292
Croûte Suisse, 305
Croque-Monsieur, 306
Croque-Madame, 306
Mussel Sandwich from Provence, 307
Bread Pudding, 323

Germany
Zwiebel Kuchen, 61
Berliner, 171
Schwarzwalder Roggen Brot, 223
Pfannkuchen fur Suppe, 288
Checkerboards, 308

Holland
Oliebollen, 172
Rusks, 174
Honey Bread, 268

Hungary
Pogacsa, 111
Sour Cream Dough, 145

Iceland
Karin's Whole-wheat Bread, 63
Laufabraud, 241

India
Chapati, 243
Mrs. Mendiratta's Lentil Chapati, 244
Cumin Balls, 245
Well-Behaved Bread, 246
Breakfast or Tea Bread, 269
Poori with a Sweet Filling, 270

Iran
Barbari Bread, 65

Ireland
Barm Brack, 176
Banbridge Oatcakes, 247
Jack and Doris Smith's Irish Soda Bread, 248

Italy
Pane Origano, 66
Pizza, 68
Pizza Napoletana, 69
Pizza Con Funghi, 69
Pizza Con Cipolle Ed Olive, 70

Grissini, 113
Maritozzi Romani, 177
Panettone, 178
Pangiallo, 180
Scripelle, 293
Guastieddi, 309
Mozzarella in Carrozza, 310

Jewish
Challah, 71
Small Poppy Seed Braids, 115
Zemmeln, 117
Onion Zemmeln, 118
Blintzes, 294

Kenya
Margaret's Sambosas, 119

Lebanon
Fatayir, 121

Liberia
Liberian Rice Bread, 271

Lithuania
Baltic Rye Bread, 224

Mexico
Panecillos, 123
Corn Bread, 249

Morocco
Whole-wheat Anise and Sesame Seed Bread, 73
Sfenj (Doughnuts), 74
Khboz Bishemar, 124

Norway
Lefse, 75
Kringler, 126
Julekake, 182
Vaniljboller, 184
Potato Lefse, 250

Poland
Sabina Bread, 77
Walnut and Poppy-seed Bread, 186

Portugal
Broa, 78
White Bread, 79
Massa Sovada, 188
Portuguese Sweet Bread, 190

Rumania
Sour Cream Dough, 145

Russia
Alma's Black Bread, 80
Romovaya Baba, 167
Kulich, 191
Ukrainian Coffee Bread, 193
Blinis, 291

Scandinavia
Scandinavian White Bread, 82

Scotland
Barra Muffins, 251
Oatcake, 252

Spain
Picatostes, 324
Spanish Toast, 325

Sweden
Fullkornsbröd, 84
Kryddlimpa, 85
Rågkakor, 87
Sur-sött Bröd, 89
Tunnbröd, 90
Bergis, 127
Frukostgifflar, 129
Blåbärskaka, 195
Bullar, 197
Fettisdagsbullar, 199
Kanelbrod, 201
Kryddskorpor, 203
Lussekatter, 205
Saffron Cardamon Braid, 207
Skokladgiffel, 209
Slottskringlor, 211
Medeltida Bröd, 226
Surmjölksbröd, 253
Hastbullar, 272
Pepparkaka, 273
Blinis, 291
Gräddvafflor, 295
Morotspannkakor, 296
Plattar, 297
Applekalle, 311
Caviar Sandwich, 312
Grilled Salami Sandwich, 313
Grilled Swiss Cheese Sandwich, 314
Ölsmorgas, 315
Fattigmans Middag, 326

Switzerland
Birnenwecken, 212
Swiss Apple and Bread Dessert, 327

Thailand
Coconut Pancakes, 298

Trinidad
Pumpkin Bread, 92

Turkey
Chicken Borek, 130
Spicy Almond Bread, 275

United States
Dill Bread, 93
Plain All-purpose Yeast Dough, 94
Herb Bread, 95
Ruth's Peanut Butter Bread, 97
Ruth's Pear and Date Bread, 99
Seven Grain Bread, 100
English Muffins, 131
Georgia Raised Biscuits, 133
Cloverleaf Rolls, 134
Parker House Rolls, 135
Pretzels, 136
Southern Potato Rolls, 137
Hot Cross Buns, 162
Bourbon Sticky Buns, 214
Cinnamon Rolls, 216
Plain White Sourdough Bread, 227
Sourdough Butter Rolls, 228
Sourdough Pancakes, 229
Boston Brown Bread, 254
Cornsticks, 255
Cream Cheese Biscuits, 256
New England Bran Muffins, 257
Popovers, 258
Southern Sweet Potato Bread, 259
Spoon Bread, 260
Blueberry Muffins, 276
Corn Muffins with Orange, 277
Philpy, 278
Pecan Bread, 279
Basic Mix for Pancakes and Waffles, American-Style (I), 286
Thin Pancakes with Meat, Sea Food or Vegetable Filling, 290
Pancakes or Waffles American-Style (II), 299
Garlic-Parmesan Bread, 328
Italian-style Bread Crumbs, 329

West Africa
Rice Bread, 280

Yugoslavia
Beogradska Pita, 281

ABOUT THE AUTHOR

A member of an international bread-loving family, Mariana Honig traces her early interest in bread baking to her childhood days in Sweden, where she learned the culinary arts under the tutelage of her mother. She continued her studies in France and Italy, where she was sent on assignment as the youngest reporter for one of Scandinavia's most prestigious newspapers.

An entrepreneur in the import-export field, Ms. Honig is President of Trans Bahari Corp., a firm specializing in African and European luxury goods and crafts. Traveling extensively for business and pleasure, Ms. Honig has collected hundreds of the better bread recipes from around the world, and compiled them with an eye towards ease in preparation, availability of ingredients, and of course, the tastiest results.

Mariana Honig currently resides in New York with her husband and three children.